EXPOSING JEZEBEL

A Manual to Unmask and Defeat the Spirit of Witchcraft

Rhonda Amsterdam

"Exposing Jezebel—A Manual to Unmask and Defeat the Spirit of Witchcraft" by Rhonda Amsterdam

Cover design, editing, book layout, and publishing services by Kish-Knows, Inc., Richton Park, Illinois, 708-252-DOIT

admin@kishknows.com, www.kishknows.com

ISBN 978-0-578-66335-7
LCCN 2020904840

All rights reserved. No part of this book may be reproduced, distributed, or transmitted in any form or by any means, including photocopying, recording, digital scanning, or other electronic or mechanical methods, without the prior written permission of the publisher, except in the case of brief quotations embodied in critical reviews and certain other noncommercial uses permitted by copyright law. For permission requests, please contact Rhonda Amsterdam.

Some Scripture references may be paraphrased versions or illustrative references of the author. All other references are specified KJV (King James Version), NKJV (New King James Version), or NIV (New International Version).

Copyright © 2020 by Rhonda Amsterdam

Printed in the United States of America

Table of Contents

Foreword v

Preface vii

Chapter 1: Witchcraft: A Work of the Flesh 1

Chapter 2: Jezebel 7

Chapter 3: Ahab: A Match Made in Demonic Heaven 30

Chapter 4: Weapons and Tactics of Jezebel 41

Chapter 5: Witchcraft in the Church 55

Chapter 6: Witchcraft in the Family 69

Chapter 7: Getting to the Roots 78

Chapter 8: The Spirit of Jezebel and Feminism 83

Chapter 9: Defeating the Demon of Witchcraft 95

Acknowledgments 104

About the Author 105

Contact the Author 106

Foreword

Why another book on "Jezebel"? you might ask. Truth is, we'll never get tired of reading it because the devil doesn't have only one plan to pull his strings. Once we discover his plots, he strategizes again—and then launches. The more we discover his antics, the more he launches his new plans. You probably think you know all there is to Jezebel until you hear the next story.

I have always taught that this is an era in which unprecedented revival is about to burst forth on the earth, but I never complete that statement without saying, "So lies a great rebellion." For every wheat, there's an opposing tare.

You see, as much as evil tries to silence godly counsels, godly wisdom, and godly principles, the Truth will always prevail. The kingdom of light will always win. The devil is fighting a lost battle. His strategy is distraction and deception, as he uses his cohorts to manipulate and cause havoc on the earth.

Prophetess Rhonda is one whom I consider as one of the most refreshing prophetic voices in this season. She's definitely one of the most trusted voices I have encountered with a heart for kingdom and deliverance. Prophetess Rhonda is an avid learner and a committed student to the text of Scriptures. I would call her a Bible lover, and this is the reason I am happy to write the foreword to this wonderful piece.

In the midst of a rising rebellious movement in the Body of Christ, which of course is a seed sown by demonic powers, we are privy to the instrumentality of Satan's plot to thwart God's prophetic plan for HIS Bride. It is a season of great apostasy and capturing the minds of the vulnerable by implanting Jezebelic and demonic systems in place to distract the believer from fulfilling their prophetic assignment on the earth. Prophetess Rhonda captures the times and seasons and the spirit of the hour.

It is with great pleasure, and I am quite frankly happy to do a foreword for this work. I have seen Prophetess Rhonda practice what she teaches, and her heart for a righteous and godly cause to prevail is quite an admirable gesture. After much thought on this masterpiece, I am fully convinced this is not just a book written to unveil the agenda of Jezebel, but provide strategic warfare against the systems of hell.

Prophetess Rhonda has taken time to underscore the need for the Church to know who they are in Christ in order to contend the power of hell. This book is written to empower you and equip you against the prevailing evil of this hour. This book thoroughly deals with witchcraft in the Church, witchcraft in the family, and the tactics and weapons of Jezebel.

For me, one of the most exciting parts of this book is when Prophetess Rhonda went to the roots of Jezebelic agenda and also destroying the works of witchcraft. This book will provoke you to intercession and make you press into a deeper realm of Christ where our victory has been made certain. I admonish you to go through the pages of this great book patiently, and you'll be amazed at the revelatory insight written in ink.

~Dr. Oscar Guobadia, Senior Pastor, The Brook Place,
London, England

Preface

Prophets and prophetic people are no strangers to Jezebel and the witchcraft associated with this spirit. Jezebel hates prophets and, by extension, prophetic people. Some of the aforementioned will have more frequent and intense encounters than others. Both experiencing and addressing the issue of witchcraft always results in mixed reactions. Some people will be able to relate and offer solace and wisdom for dealing with such encounters. Some will tell you that you are overreacting, yet others will try to make you feel as though what you are experiencing is your fault. The thing about experience is no one can take it away from you. You experienced the pain and trauma of the encounters. Never allow people to reduce what you have experienced to ash because they have never experienced it or because someone perhaps once called them "Jezebel" and it left a bad taste in their mouth.

Life is a journey taken one experience at a time. How we respond to what we've been through will determine the quality of our journey, whether we stride forward as victors or limp away as victims. Only *we* decide. There is purpose in pain, although pain in its season feels like an abyss.

During my initial years of encountering witchcraft attacks, I felt like my journey was an abyss and gravity my only ally. I was surrounded by good people, but absolutely, no one could have detected that I was under the attack of witchcraft; and absolutely no one could have related to what I was going through. I felt alone, but I knew something was wrong. I simply did not know what it was. Now I know, now I understand, now I can discern. Now I have wisdom and insight. That is what I will give to you in this book—the wisdom and knowledge I have gathered over the years so that you can navigate your journey with less pain and be fully armed with the knowledge that you are not alone. Knowledge makes you wiser, stronger, and better positioned to prevail because you know what you are dealing with.

2 Peter 1:3 says, "as his divine power hath given unto us all things that *pertain* unto life and godliness, through the knowledge of him that hath called us to glory and virtue." You already have power and victory over Jezebel and its witchcraft. My task is to teach you how to take it. I declare in Jesus' name that your journey, your life, will be filled with glory and virtue.

Chapter 1:

Witchcraft: A Work of the Flesh

Witchcraft

Usually, when we hear about witchcraft, we think about spells, magic, incantations, and other occult activities. However, there are two aspects of witchcraft. There is the supernatural aspect which most have solely associated this word. And there is the natural aspect. The natural aspect of witchcraft comes from the carnal or uncrucified nature of man. It is soulish and built on the bedrock of self-will. It seeks to exercise control over others. Although the two aspects are different, they both find their origin in the demonic spirit realm.

Merriam Webster's Dictionary defines "witchcraft" as *the use of sorcery or magic, communication with the devil or with a familiar; an irresistible influence or fascination; Wicca*. Most, if not this entire definition, will be reflected as you continue to read. It is quite interesting that Galatians 5:19-20 lists witchcraft as a manifestation of the works of the flesh.

"Now the works of the flesh are manifest, which are these; Adultery, fornication, uncleanness, lasciviousness, idolatry, witchcraft, hatred, variance, emulations, wrath, strife, seditions, heresies."

A Work of the Flesh

Christ desires to be exalted in our lives. Therefore, our will and desires are to be governed by the Holy Spirit. However, when man chooses to be self-willed and enthroned as king in his own life, then whatever is done from this posture is a manifestation of the work of the flesh.

Both the natural man and the carnal man are ruled by their flesh. A natural man is an individual who has never surrendered their life to Christ. 1 Corinthians 2:14 says, "But the natural man does not receive the things of the Spirit of God, for they are foolishness to him; nor can he know them, because they are spiritually discerned." (NKJV) A natural man cannot receive nor discern things of the Spirit of God since the spirit of such an individual is dead. Only spirit can receive from Spirit. Because of this status of having a dead spirit, a natural man views all things spiritual as foolishness. Therefore, such individuals are controlled by their fleshly nature.

Let's always remember that man is spirit, and that he has a soul and lives in a body. The spirit of man is God-conscious. The soul of man is self-conscious. Before the fall, man lived according to his spirit, which was created God-conscious.

When Adam sinned in the Garden of Eden, his God-consciousness and his spirit that was alive, died, and self-consciousness occupied the vacuum created. Out of this state, he procreated; thus, everyone was born in this manner. Therefore, the entire human race is self-conscious rather than God-conscious. When an individual gives their life to Christ, their spirit that was dead comes alive; they become God-conscious again. Thus, they can receive and discern the things of the Spirit of God. "And you He made alive, who were dead in trespasses and sins." (Ephesians 2:1 NKJV) The state of being self-conscious rather than God-conscious is also referred to as "the old nature" and "unregenerate person."

A carnal man is a believer who does not live a life led by the Holy Spirit nor by the Word of God, but by his desire and intellect. This is the case even though such an individual had the ability to receive and discern the things of the Spirit from the moment they surrendered their life to Christ. The word "carnal" comes from the Greek word "sarkikos" and means *pertaining to the flesh, temporal, unregenerate, etc.* Thus, carnal believers function on a fleshy, unregenerate level. These are people who Apostle Paul describes as "babes in Christ." "And I, brethren, could not speak to you as to spiritual people but as to carnal, as to babes in Christ. I fed you with milk and not with solid food; for until now you were not able to receive it, and even now you are still not able; for you are still carnal. For where there are envy, strife, and divisions among you, are you not carnal and behaving like mere men?" (1 Corinthians 3:1-3 NKJV)

A life ruled by the flesh does not only negatively impact the individual who is natural or carnal but others as well, since the enemy can use such an individual as a channel through which he targets and attacks believers who are continuously surrendered and are growing in their relationship with God.

Surrendering our lives to Christ is never a one-time occasion but a continuous lifestyle. We need to live surrendered lives, never retreating to our old ways. Fruit of the Holy Spirit such as love, joy, peace, kindness, patience, and so on are evidence of continuous surrender and spiritual growth. An individual who is surrendered does not remain in a state of struggling with elementary things such as strife, hate, divisions, and the like. This is the challenge the Apostle Paul was having with the believers in the church at Corinth. The aforementioned is the struggle many leaders still have today. Believers are in church for most of their adult life but are still struggling with elementary, fleshly issues; still living a life led by their unregenerate nature.

Witchcraft, as a manifestation of the work of the flesh is the flesh in control. Anyone who functions from the natural aspect of witchcraft will seek to exercise control over others. Exercising control over the will of another is wrong because God created man with free will. This is clearly reflected in Genesis 2:15-17, "Then the Lord God took the man and put him in the Garden of Eden to tend and keep it. And the Lord God commanded the man, saying, 'Of every tree of the garden you may freely eat; but of the tree of the knowledge of good and evil you shall not eat, for in the day that you eat of it you shall surely die.'" (NKJV) Adam was given a clear commandment and a clear consequence if he disobeyed. We all know that Adam disobeyed that commandment. His disobedience resulted in all of humanity being born slaves to a sinful nature. However, when Jesus Christ died on the cross, he restored the opportunity for all humanity to live as free moral agents. We can choose to serve Christ or not. All of our relationships should afford others this kind of freedom. A person operating in witchcraft removes or seeks to remove free will from another person and exercise illegitimate authority.

Witchcraft is a manifestation of the work of the flesh. It is often difficult to detect this controlling spirit as it's a master at intertwining itself into the personality of the individual through whom it works. Often, we see a controlling person and hear people say, "that's just the way he is," or "that's just the way she is" but it's more than that. Although the manifestations of this spirit are often challenging to detect, someone who has experience confronting such a spirit can recognize it quickly. As you continue to read, you will be able to identify this spirit easily as well. Just like an individual who performs any other work of the flesh such as hate, envy, strife, fornication, and murder, a person who functions out of witchcraft is not necessarily demonized, but their behavior is demonic because the demonic spirit realm influences it.

We must always be conscious of the fact that two different and opposing spirits influence everyone in this world and that there is no neutral zone. Consequently, every individual either lives a life led by the Holy Spirit or the one who the Bible refers to as "the prince of the power of the air." Ephesians 2:1-3 explains this so clearly for us: "And you He made alive, who were dead in trespasses and sins, in which you once walked according to the course of this world, according to the prince of the power of the air, the spirit who now works in the sons of disobedience, among whom also we all once conducted ourselves in the lusts of our flesh, fulfilling the desires of the flesh and of the mind, and were by nature children of wrath, just as the others." (NKJV)

Self-examination is critical. If such an individual does not examine themselves and deal with the issues of their heart that give the prince of the power of the air access to work through them, then a demon, which is a spirit that functions under the leadership of the prince of the power of the air, also known as Satan, comes and sits in that place created and rules through that person. When that happens, that individual becomes demonically energized and empowered. Consequently, the witchcraft power in their life is no longer natural but supernatural.

Therefore, when someone is under attack from the natural aspect of witchcraft, it means that the devil or demons are targeting and attacking that individual through the natural or carnal nature of human beings. Simply put, one person is seeking to exercise control over another.

We know our fight is never against flesh and blood; however, we cannot effectively combat and defeat an enemy that we are unable to identify. Thus, the taunting question: Who is the strongman? What principality governs this spirit of witchcraft? "When Joram saw Jehu he asked, 'Have you come in peace, Jehu?'

'How can there be peace,' Jehu replied, 'as long as all the idolatry and witchcraft of your mother Jezebel abound?'" (2 Kings 9:22 NIV) Jezebel is that principality, that strongman, ruling over witchcraft. And similarly, to the idolatrous Old Testament queen from whom this principality got its name, Jezebel the principality, uses witchcraft against its enemies.

Reflection

1. Can those around me see the evidence of my continuous surrender to Christ and my growth in Him?
2. When in difficult situations, do I retreat to my old nature?
3. What steps should I take to ensure that I am always growing spiritually?

Prayer and Declaration

Father, in the name of Jesus, I surrender myself to You; mind, will, and emotions. Jesus, be exalted in my life each day. Holy Spirit, I am asking that You lead me continually. I surrender to You. I desire to grow from strength to strength. Grant me the grace, so that I can stand faithful to you in difficult situations, never retreating to my old way of life. In Jesus' name. Amen.

Chapter 2:

Jezebel

Jezebel, the Phoenician Princess

This Phoenician princess sprang from a pagan root; she was the daughter of Ethbaal, king of the Sidonians. The Phoenicians worshipped Baal and Ashtoreth or Astarte. Her father was a high priest of Baal. His very name boldly proclaimed his posture as it relates to worship. "Ethbaal" meant *with Baal*.

Jezebel was a zealous idolater and dedicated worshipper of Baal. Even her name Jeze "bel" rang this reality. This Baal devotee was committed to establishing Baal worship in Israel amongst God's chosen ones. To this end, a magnificent temple was built in Samaria and furnished with a large number of priests. On the other hand, she relentlessly tried to exterminate the worship of the true and living God by driving out and murdering the true prophets of God. Thereby she encrypted herself in history as the first known female religious persecutor. Jezebel would have prevailed had God not inserted Obadiah, Elijah, and Jehu in at just the right time during this wicked queen's reign.

Based on the events in the Bible in which she was prominent, the facts are irrefutable. Jezebel was anything but average. Ruthless, vicious, and proud, she strutted the halls of time, leaving no impression of a woman who possessed any admirable or replicable qualities.

Lineage of the Gods Jezebel Worshipped

Very present, in almost every strand of society, is Jezebel that principality which now bears the name of the Phoenician princess and ancient Israelite queen. In order for us to understand the workings and manifestations of the aforementioned, it is imperative that we have an understanding of the gods that Jezebel, the woman, worshipped, since the principality and demon now bears their nature.

Pagan Gods of the Other Nations

The Bible is not shy in unveiling the fact that the nations which existed in antiquity worshipped other gods. It is quite evident in the Old Testament. It appears as though each nation had its national god. However, a nation also worshipped the gods of other nations, especially if they were conquered by or came into an alliance with that nation. And if a god was believed to rule a territory.

Chemosh was the national god of Moab. They were called "people of Chemosh" as seen in Numbers 21:29, "Woe to you, Moab! You are destroyed, people of Chemosh! He has given up his sons as fugitives and his daughters as captives to Sihon, king of the Amorites. Moab also worshipped Molech and Milcom.

Dagon was the national god of the Philistines. "Now the rulers of the Philistines assembled to offer a great sacrifice to Dagon their god and to celebrate, saying, "Our god has delivered Samson, our enemy, into out hands," Judges 16:23.

Egypt worshipped a pantheon of gods and goddesses such as Ra, Osiris, Horis, Mut, Maat. "For I will pass through the land of Egypt that night, and I will strike all the firstborn in the land of Egypt, both man and beast; and on all the gods of Egypt I will execute judgments: I am the Lord," Exodus 12:12.

Tamzu was a Syrian god. "Then he brought me to the entrance of the north gate of the house of the Lord, and I saw women sitting there, mourning the god Tammuz." Ezekiel 8:14

In the New Testament era, Greek goddess Artemis aka Diana was worshipped at Ephesus and other places. "There is danger not only that our trade will lose its good name, but also that the temple of the great goddess Artemis will be discredited; and the goddess herself, who is worshipped throughout the providence of Asia and the world, will be robbed of her divine majesty." Acts 19:27

The Sidionians worshipped Baal and Ashtoreth. Jezebel's father, Ethbaal, was a high priest of Baal. It was believed that Jezebel was a high priestess of this deity. The high priests were believed to interact directly with these demonic deities. Hence, these deities usually shared secrets with them. Thus, those serving these deities in this capacity understood the agenda of the gods they worshipped. I know, we who are in a charismatic movement like to comfort or even delude ourselves into thinking that those who worship "idols" or false gods worship mere lifeless objects.

However, as I said, we have deluded ourselves furthermore I pray that we continue to be delivered from this delusion. The gods that the nations around Israel worshipped were more than mere stones or "idols." As a matter of fact, in antiquity, where "idols" existed, it was understood that those objects were not gods. Rather those were places where the gods were made local or a place prepared for the gods to dwell, receive worship, sacrifices, and so on. Hence, they performed ceremonies to "open the mouth" of the statue. The mouth and nostrils had to be ritually opened for the deity to "inhabit" the statue.

Whenever you see idolatry mentioned in the Bible, always think of it in terms of the worship of something or someone other than the "I AM," the God of Abraham, Isaac, and Jacob, the Creator of the heavens and earth; Yahweh is the covenant name of the God of Israel under the old covenant. And the God Head or Triune God under the New Covenant; Father, Son and Holy Spirit.

We see the worship of Baal and Ashtoreth from Genesis to Revelation. They are known in different nations and eras by various aliases; Baal is known as El, Bel, Beelzebub, and Baal with all of its hyphenations and variations. Ashtoreth is known as Astarte, Queen of Heaven, Ishtar, Isis, Whore of Babylon in the Book of Revelation, Virgin Mary, and Lady of Fatima.

In his book, *Jezebel, Seducing Goddess of War*, Jonas Clark states the following on page 73: "Ashtoreth is identified with several different names through history worth noting, including "bride of heaven," "goddess of holiness," and "goddess of good fortune." She was also known as the "queen of heaven," a title Catholics use for Mary, Jesus' mother. Ashtoreth is also called by several other names including Astarte, Ishtar, Ashtart, Asherah and Aphrodite. Whatever you prefer to call her, Ashtoreth and the spirit of Jezebel are one and the same." By the time Jezebel, the human came on the scene, Baal was a Phoenician sun god whose name means "owner, lord, master, husband." The word is also used to imply ownership of traits or possession of things. Baal is depicted as half bull, half man. This deity was believed to be highly adaptable, and different groups worshipped Baal in different ways. Baal was also believed to possess powers in many areas such as fertility, control of weather and seasons, and so on.

The Principal Pillars of Baal Worship

Child sacrifice: during this practice live infants were burnt in the hands of the statue of Baal, while worshippers indulged in sexual orgies which often resulted in unwanted pregnancies. These pregnancies, however, produced a supply of infants for sacrifice.

Sexual immorality is another pillar of Baal worship; both heterosexual and homosexual.

The god of nature: Baal was believed to have total control over nature. Hence, child sacrifices were made for good weather, bountiful crops, and other favors.

Baal Worship in Today's Culture and Systems

Child sacrifice: this has been renamed "abortion" today and touted as "Pro-choice" which is, of course, the worship of self-will.

Sexual immorality: desperate attempts are being made to normalize the ritualistic practice and celebration of both heterosexual and homosexual practices and other forms of immorality.

The god of nature: now worshipped via pantheism; which holds the view that everything is god and god is everything. Thus, the love for "Mother Earth" which is seen in radical environmentalism. Pantheism is shown in the worship of nature, praying to the universe and revering the creation over the Creator.

I strongly believe that humanity should be responsible stewards of the earth. However, the depopulation agenda, in its many forms, is also a manifestation of the spirit of Jezebel. Humanity is not squatting on this planet. We were assigned to live here by the creator of the earth. There is enough space and resource for everyone.

Ashtoreth or Astarte

This is a female deity connected with fertility, sexuality, and war. She is referred to as "Queen of Heaven" in Jeremiah 7:16-18 and Jeremiah 44:17-25. Several symbols depict this deity, including the lion and the dove. She is often portrayed as nude, sometimes pregnant and with exaggerated breasts that she holds out. The priests and priestesses of Ashtoreth practiced divination and fortune-telling. Both male and female prostitutes worshipped in the temple of this fertility god. Acts of worship included sexual orgies and promiscuity. Sexual perversion was prevalent.

Baal and Ashtoreth were sun and moon deities. They were said to function from the second heaven and were believed to come under the direct authority of Satan. Because of their union, they displayed similar traits, and they both controlled information. Thus, this is the source from which psychics, palm readers, tarot card readers, fortune tellers, false and diviner prophetic voices (Balaam prophets), and those who operate in clairvoyance, familiar spirits, and the like obtain information. Thus, Jezebel has a prophetic voice. Because of this, prophetic accuracy should not be the only standard used to measure the authenticity of prophetic utterances. The source of a prophetic utterance is as important as the accuracy.

Realms and Dimensions

Who gives the information? Just because someone heard something from the spirit realm, it does not necessarily mean that God spoke to them. Authentic prophecy comes from the third heaven, where the throne of God is situated. The Cambridge Dictionary defines "dimensions" as *a measurement of something in a particular direction, especially its height, length, or width.* Genesis 1:1 tells us, "In the beginning God created the heavens and the earth." (NIV) We know that the earth has dimensions: height, length, width, and depth. This means that, like the earth, the heavens which were also created have dimensions too. Further, let's note that "heavens" is in the plural and "earth" is in the singular. Therefore, there is one earth but more than one heaven.

In general, it is accepted that there are three heavens, and here is why. 2 Corinthians 12:2-4 states, "I know a man in Christ who fourteen years ago whether in the body I do not know, or whether out of the body I do not know, God knows—such a one was caught up to the third heaven. And I know such a man whether in the body or out of the body I do not know, God knows how he was caught up into Paradise and heard inexpressible words, which it is not lawful for a man to utter." (NKJV) Hebrews 8:1 states, "Now *this is* the main point of the things we are saying: We have such a High Priest, who is seated at the right hand of the throne of the Majesty in the heavens." (NKJV)

Jezebel

These two Scriptures disclose that there is a third heaven and that it's the place where God resides. Since there is a third heaven, it's only practical that there is a second and first.

The second heaven is believed to be the celestial or stellar heaven. Deuteronomy 4:19 supports a stellar heaven. "And take heed, lest you lift your eyes to heaven, and when you see the sun, the moon, and the stars, all the host of heaven, you feel driven to worship them and serve them, which the Lord your God has given to all the peoples under the whole heaven as a heritage." (NKJV)

Ephesians 6:12 supports the belief that the second heaven is the celestial heaven or the demonic dimension. "For we do not wrestle against flesh and blood, but against principalities, against powers, against the rulers of the darkness of this age, against spiritual *hosts of wickedness in the heavenly places.*" (NKJV) This belief is further strengthened by Daniel 10:12-14 and Ephesians 2:2. The latter Scripture refers to a celestial being as "the prince of the power of the air." This being is acknowledged to be Satan. Thus, Satan has his kingdom set up in the second heaven. I believe Baal and Ashtoreth are principal spirits in Satan's kingdom; thus, they too reside in the second heaven.

The first heaven is the atmospheric heaven which includes the air we breathe and the atmosphere immediately surrounding the earth.

The difference between a realm and a dimension is this: the term "dimension" refers to *the measurement of a space* while the KJV dictionary defines "realm" as *a royal jurisdiction or extent of government; a kingdom, a king's dominions, as the realm of England, kingly government.* With those two words now clarified, we can see that Satan's jurisdiction and kingdom are in the second heaven or that which is referred to as "the demonic realm." Jesus Christ, the throne of God, and angelic beings reside in the third heaven or that which can be called "the throne of God."

Since Baal and Ashtoreth are seated in the second heaven, they too can, therefore, access and communicate accurate information to their agents. Genuine prophetic voices can receive information from the second heaven. The aforementioned is possible when prophetic voices love the gift of prophecy more than the giver of the gift, who is the Holy Spirit. This can also happen when their level of intimacy with the Lord is low. We can only know and keep knowing the voice of the Lord through intimacy with Him. When very little time is spent with the Lord, you may not be able to distinguish other voices from His; but because you are receiving information, you may think it's from Him. You may be wondering why the devil would want to give you accurate information. The devil's ultimate goal is to deceive. However, he will draw you in by telling you what you want to hear.

The Principality

As a principality, Jezebel takes on the status and traits of both Baal and Ashtoreth. This principality is territorial; it governs and influences regions, nations, systems and cultures within nations, people groups, and organizations. Therefore, wherever there are practices and belief systems as such that are previously listed in connection with Baal and Ashtoreth, know that Jezebel; the principality, is the force influencing it.

"For we do not wrestle against flesh and blood, but against principalities, against powers, against the rulers of the darkness of this age, against spiritual *hosts* of wickedness in the heavenly *places.*" (Ephesians 6:12 NKJV) Merriam Webster Dictionary defines "principality" as *the state, office, or authority of a prince.* And "principalities" as *an order of angels.* I love the satanic hierarchy Kimberly Daniels has in her book *Give It Back.* Below is an excerpt.

Satan – the prince of the power of the air

Beelzebub – the prince of devils – answers directly to Satan

Principalities – princes of the four corners of the earth (continents, countries, state, cities, counties), arch magistrates or principal demons; first in rank

Power – organizations (*exousia* – special ability, highly competent; liberty in jurisdiction)

Ruler spirits – neighborhoods, families, individuals, (*kosmokrator* – world ruler, spirits with direct contact with their targets)

Spiritual wickedness in high places – idolatry (Hezekiah tore down the high places) (*poneria*- iniquity and malice, sin and idolatrous activity.)"

I will make a tiny adjustment to this hierarchy for the purpose of this book. In my version, I will replace "Beelzebub" with "Baal" and "Ashtoreth." I am of the belief that Baal and Beelzebub are one and the same. The reason I placed Ashtoreth beside Baal is because the two function in unison. Here is the tweaked version:

Satan – the prince of the power of the air

Baal and Ashtoreth (Baal aka Beelzebub) – the prince of devils – answers directly to Satan

Principalities – princes of the four corners of the earth (continents, countries, state, cities, counties), arch magistrates or principal demons; first in rank. E.g. **Jezebel**

Power – organizations (*exousia* –special ability, highly competent; liberty in jurisdiction)

Ruler spirits – neighborhoods, families, individuals, (*kosmokrator* – world ruler, spirits with direct contact with their targets

Spiritual wickedness in high places – idolatry (Hezekiah tore down the high places) (*poneria-* iniquity and malice, sin, and idolatrous activity.)

The name "Babylon" came from the word "Babel." Babylon was a city with a tower that was created as an act of rebellion against Yahweh. Babylon is now the world system that stands in opposition to Yahweh with Jezebel enthroned as queen, falling under the demonic hierarchy of Baal and Ashtoreth. However, there is a prophetic word out concerning Jezebel, "And another angel followed, saying, 'Babylon is fallen, is fallen, that great city, because she has made all nations drink of the wine of the wrath of her fornication'" (Revelation 14:8 NKJV) And again, "Then one of the seven angels who had the seven bowls came and talked with me, saying to me, 'Come, I will show you the judgment of the great harlot who sits on many waters, with whom the kings of the earth committed fornication, and the inhabitants of the earth were made drunk with the wine of her fornication.' So, he carried me away in the Spirit into the wilderness. And I saw a woman sitting on a scarlet beast *which was* full of names of blasphemy, having seven heads and ten horns. The woman was arrayed in purple and scarlet, and adorned with gold and precious stones and pearls, having in her hand a golden cup full of abominations and the filthiness of her fornication. And on her forehead a name *was* written: MYSTERY, BABYLON THE GREAT, THE MOTHER OF HARLOTS AND OF THE ABOMINATIONS OF THE EARTH. I saw the woman, drunk with the blood of the saints and with the blood of the martyrs of Jesus. And when I saw her, I marveled with great amazement" (Revelation 17:1-6 NKJV)

Jezebel Demons

I believe that Jezebel the principality has foot soldiers; mini Jezebel demons assigned to it. These demons manifest themselves through the worship of self-will. If our wills are not surrendered to the authority of the Word of God and the Holy Spirit, then we are worshipping our self-will. The worship of self-will is the manifestation of a Jezebel spirit and ultimately the worship of Baal and an act of rebellion against Yahweh.

People who worship self-will will also seek to exercise control over the will of others. This is witchcraft. Those who behave in this manner are said to have a spirit of Jezebel, or they are simply referred to as Jezebels. However, it is critical that we remember Ephesians 6:12, "For we wrestle not against flesh and blood, but against principalities, against powers, against the rulers of the darkness of this world, against spiritual wickedness in high places." (KJV)

What a Jezebel Spirit Is Not

There are still many misconceptions concerning the Jezebel spirit. Thus, I will focus firstly on who is not Jezebel.

- The devil has been successful in deceiving us into thinking that Jezebel is about hair, makeup, and clothing. Jezebel is not the sister who dresses provocatively and who wears a lot of makeup, or the sister who is continuously seeking the pastor or an elder's attention. Such individuals may have issues and may indeed need love, prayer, counsel, and support but they do not need the negative labeling.
- Jezebel is not that bold, outspoken woman. God created bold, outspoken individuals in both the male and female genders. It is unfortunate to note that there are still men who are uncomfortable with and who are intimidated by females who are not docile, reserved, or soft-spoken. Thus, they seek to shut down such women with this evil label.
- Jezebel is not a woman who is more influential or may have a stronger grace to publicly lead than her husband. More and more, we see married women taking up their God-given roles of leading movements and ministries. This, however, does not indicate that the woman is in charge of the marriage. I believe that if a woman understands and teaches herself to adjust in her roles as wife in the home and leader in ministry or career, her

marital relationship can flow excellently. Also, a wise woman will understand that she can function in authority in public life only to the extent that she submits to her husband's authority in the marriage. Deborah, one of the judges of Israel, is an excellent example of a married woman with a prominent public role. "Now Deborah, a prophetess, the wife of Lapidoth, was judging Israel at that time. And she would sit under the palm tree of Deborah between Ramah and Bethel in the mountains of Ephraim. And the children of Israel came up to her for judgment." (Judges 4:4-5 NKJV)

- Also, there is a tendency to associate the spirit of Jezebel with females. This too is incorrect. The Oxford Dictionary defines "spirit" as *a supernatural being*. Thus, spirits are gender-neutral, and both males and females can come under the influence of this spirit. Although this spirit is more prevalent in women, it functions a bit differently but just as proficiently in men.

Unhusbanded

The name Jezebel means *unexalted* or *unhusbanded*. Unhusbanded is the past tense of married. This word also implies the unreserved and uneconomic use of resources. Jezebels are committed to no one but themselves and their agendas. They desire the rewards associated with a stable, committed relationship while remaining uncommitted. They will lay claim to the influence and opportunities that may be associated with their connections but will resist any form of refining, rebuke, or correction that may be required.

Being joined to a leader is usually superficial; such an individual will disconnect once they realize that they are unable to reap the type of benefit perceived. Such individuals may frequently change spiritual fathers and leaders, and they may have several spiritual fathers.

Even when such individuals are in positions of leadership, they have a "taker" mentality. The flow between their relationships is usually tilted so that they are continually receiving. For this reason, such a leader may try to have stronger relational ties to members with money, social, or political influence. This is also the reason individuals may feel used after severing ties with such a leader.

Too often, leaders swing the doors wide open for the unhusbanded when they are too anxious to place new people in positions and assign tasks, especially if these individuals are talented or qualified in areas of need in the church. Sometimes, Jezebel shows up as an answer to prayers. For this reason, leaders need to exercise patience, test the spirits, and hear what the Lord has to say concerning an individual. Do not work on impulse and do not make decisions based only on need. Allowing people to show commitment to the vision of the church without any assigned tasks and positions could save much headache and heartache. I believe this is the reason the Apostle Paul told Timothy, his son in the faith, "And the things that you have heard from me among many witnesses, commit these to faithful men who will be able to teach others also." (2 Timothy 2:2 NKJV)

The Personalities of Jezebel

As mentioned earlier, the demon-god, Ashtoreth, was depicted by several symbols, two of which included a lion and a dove. I've observed that the spirit of Jezebel tends to function out of these two personalities, particularly in women.

A lion: The lion personality Jezebel is usually a friendly, winsome, outspoken, and highly visible female. She possesses strong leadership skills and is very influential and very confident. She is an Alfa personality. She will come into a relationship with you being in control from the beginning. It may not be obvious at first because she is delivering your needs and grooming you to be dependent on her at the same time.

If confronted, she lies and denies. She finds someone to blame and plays the victim. It's useless confronting such a person, and it may be wiser to simply walk away.

A dove: The dove personality Jezebel is quite different. She presents the illusion of being kind, considerate, very submissive, and even fragile at times. She is always eager to volunteer to do something. She is dedicated to details and will give you precisely what you request. She will win your confidence but undermine and misrepresent you in the background. She is very agreeable with you in person but will question and attempt to manipulate your decisions through others. Detecting this type of Jezebel personality require discernment.

Sometimes, people will give you feedback regarding how such an individual is misrepresenting you to others, but the information you receive would seemingly not match the personality of the individual with whom you interact. If you are not discerning, you will doubt the information presented to you.

Because of her dual personalities, she can turn those, even in your close circle who only know her gentle side, against you. The aforementioned is sufficient to conclude that the dove personality Jezebel is most dangerous because she is very manipulative, most difficult to discern, and in most cases is recognized after she has done considerable damage. Boldly confront her, and her real personality will show.

Shape shifts: A Jezebel usually possesses the dominant personality of a lion or a dove. However, often, they can metamorphize from their dominant personality, temporarily, to achieve a specific goal.

The Male Jezebel

Someone I know had a traumatic encounter with the spirit of Jezebel via a male. He was an apostle and a very influential spiritual leader. She met him and his wife while attending a conference overseas. He was friendly, outgoing, and winsome. His wife was somewhat reserved but very loving and pleasant. This couple reached out to this person, and they formed a friendship which resulted in her family migrating to that country to work with this couple.

Just before migrating, a friend warned her about this man. "Be careful," she said, "he has a bad reputation regarding women and money." The woman heeded the warning but still proceeded with plans for migration as she needed to be in a new environment. She promised herself to be very careful.

Upon migrating, she and her husband began working for this couple. Everything relating to the husband was fine, but the woman had a problem. She was always on time, usually having lunch at her desk. She worked beyond closing hours, way into the evenings. She could never leave the desk to go to lunch because this apostle would come looking for her and find a task for her to do during her lunchtime. Worst of all, she was horribly underpaid.

She made several attempts to have a meeting with this couple regarding her salary, but they always found an excuse not to meet with her. After pushing, she was finally able to have a meeting. The wife seemed to agree with her dissatisfaction and indicated that they had plans to increase her salary when they could afford it. However, they were always travelling and living an outlandish lifestyle, so the excuse made no sense to this woman. She was not the only one with salary woes. Almost all of the staff had similar complaints.

After her complaint, the husband's attitude changed towards her. He began making accusations and telling lies about the woman. She confronted him and his wife about this, and they both denied the stories. He continued. Unfortunately, he was influential: he ran a business, and he was an apostle. The woman was just someone who worked for him. Those he scandalized her believed everything he said.

These people were not only her employers but her spiritual leaders. His wife was gracious; she recognized the prophetic call on this woman's life and tried to mentor her and give her room to function. The husband always tried to get in the way. In the church, the woman led worship, among other things. When it was her time to lead, he would wait until the worship was ready to start and then give her a list of songs to use. This completely threw her off, because the team had already practiced other songs, but she usually made the adjustment and worked with his list. One day, the woman finally confronted him about this and about his overall attitude towards her. She was taken off the worship team!

During the course of time, his wife died. Before she had died, she had begun to include this woman on the preaching schedule. After she had died and it was this woman's turn to preach, he called her the Saturday night before the Sunday morning to tell her she need to preach in the morning. At first, she would tell him the notice was too short, then she began preparing in advance, so she always had a message ready.

According to this woman, this Jezebelic apostle often misinterpreted and misquoted Scriptures. If people in the church had differing interpretations of a Scripture, he would tell them all that they were all correct! This woman expressed her disagreement with this approach to Bible studies on several occasions. Finally, at a leadership meeting, she raised it again. She suggested that someone teach on the topic before the discussions or explain the Scriptures relating to the discussions afterwards so that the people correctly understood the Word of God; but unfortunately, the apostle disagreed.

The warning that the woman had at the beginning concerning this apostle, money, and women turned out to be true. He handled finances poorly, constantly borrowed, and stole money from his business. He was flirtatious and a chronic cheater. Sometimes, he would take money from his business and give it to these other women of his.

Then one day, a mini-Jezebel joined this church. This apostle and her bonded immediately. She claimed to be prophetic and she always had a "word from the Lord." She gained popularity quickly.

The woman and her family eventually left that church, and I have often wondered why she didn't leave earlier.

Traits of a Male Jezebel

- The male Jezebel is very promiscuous. For some reason, he thinks he is God's gift to women. Believer or not, promiscuity is a common trait.
- He is a pathological liar. This type of individual will lie in your presence. If you challenge their story, they will change it right there and deny saying what they said just a few minutes ago. They don't mind making you think you are crazy.
- He is often charismatic.
- He is deceptive and will flatter you to the face and discredit you behind your back.
- He fakes integrity.
- He tends to twist and misinterpret Scriptures.
- He projects his weaknesses. He will accuse you of things he is guilty of, then ruthlessly scandalize you concerning it.
- He will whip out his favorite lie against you whenever you disagree with him or he figures you will attempt to expose him.
- He plays the victim, then stirs his loyalists to gang up on you.
- He will allow your reputation to be destroyed without a flicker of remorse.
- He can conjure up the appropriate emotions to accompany a fake incident.
- His victims suffer mental and financial devastation.
- If confronted, he will never take responsibility.
- He will attempt to frustrate you spiritually and make you feel inadequate.
- Because of his spiritual status, charisma, or influence, people tend to accept his stories about you without question.

- He is not open to correction.
- He is bold and ruthless.

Traits of the Spirit of Jezebel

- **Jezebel is a controller.** To avoid confusion, let me say that not all controllers are Jezebels. Some people like to control their own lives and space. That's not a Jezebel. Jezebels like to control the lives of others. They will relentlessly find avenues to manipulate situations so that they can exercise control over others. Those whom they cannot control, they will seek to destroy.
- **Jezebel chameleons.** This spirit can adapt to resemble the personality of the individual through whom it works. This is the reason it's often difficult to detect.
- **It's all about dominion.** This spirit wants to rule over people—God's people—to be specific.
- **Is genderless.** This spirit can function in both the male and female gender but is more prevalent in females.
- **Jezebel uses illegitimate authority.** Even though an individual may seem to have authority in the natural, if there is a Jezebel in their life, the posture of being in authority is just a façade. Jezebel is calling the shots in the background. This is something we need to understand about this spirit. It's not overly concerned about occupying the seat of power. The spirit is more concerned about controlling the person who occupies the seat of power.
- **This spirit will grab and own relinquished authority.** This spirit will seek opportunities to act or speak on behalf of another without authentic authorization.
- **Jezebel's presence increases wickedness.** (See 1 Kings 16:30.) Whatever diabolic strategy the enemy is using against you, when a Jezebel is present, it will be amped-up. The strategies of Jezebel will be discussed in a later chapter.
- **A false prophetic spirit.** Jezebel can give you an accurate prophetic word. Accuracy alone should never be the test of a genuine prophetic word—the source is as critical as the word. Remember, Jezebel the principality is also called the Queen

of Heaven. Thus, this spirit exists in the realm of information. Therefore, people who have a spirit of Jezebel can access information. This access, however, is illegal. The Holy Spirit is the only legal means through which anyone should gain access to the spirit realm. Also, the information Jezebel gives is usually limited. Jezebel prophesies to *inform* not *transform* you into being more like Christ. As a matter of fact, prophecies from Jezebel will strengthen demonic strongholds in your life. Jezebel's prophecies will not deal with the issues of sin in your life, and Jezebel is unable to give you accurate information concerning your destiny.

- **Clairvoyance.** Also, someone with the Jezebel spirit will have information about situations and people and tend to know exactly when to show up. Oftentimes, the individuals themselves don't understand how they know what they know. It's clairvoyance and it's demonic.
- **A self-proclaimed prophet.** (See Revelation 2:20.) With all the fake prophetic markers, it's no surprise that this spirit will proclaim itself a prophet.
- **Jezebel likes to teach and make disciples**. Jezebel will seek weak, broken, and rebellious believers to disciple. In many cases, it will be situations in which like spirits attract one another with a Jezebel leading the pack away from a Christ-centered lifestyle, from God-ordained leadership and destinies.
- **Jezebel should not be tolerated**. Never try to coexist with this spirit. In wisdom and with precise timing, this spirit has to be boldly confronted and removed from its high place.
- **Jezebel loves strife**. This spirit will set people against one another. A leader who has a Jezebel spirit will lead with a *divide and conquer* mentality. They will employ various tactics to keep those they lead suspicious of and separated from one another.
- **They love to use other people to do their dirty work while they stay at a safe distance in the background**. In this way, they remain in good relationship with both the villain they sent; who in most cases is unsuspecting, and the victim who has to receive the attack. Staying in the background keeps them in control. When the situation goes bad, they eagerly step in to make peace and bring reconciliation.

- **Jezebel is a relationship spoiler and contaminator.** Jezebel will spoil and contaminate good relationships by creating strife and suspicion, particularly among those who are young in the Lord and those not very strong in the Word. This spirit must be boldly confronted. There are different strategies for dealing with a relationship spoiler. The strategy used when the relationship is being spoilt by a leader is different from the strategy used when the spoiler is a church member. I will address both in later chapters. A couple I am acquainted with shared an experience they had when a young man joined their church. This young man was not new to church life. They discerned the call on his life to shepherd God's people. Thus, they began challenging him to step into his destiny. He was transitioning from a church in which he had been sitting, doing nothing to a church in which he was being challenged to step into his destiny, when this Jezebel woman connected to him. They started a relationship. She was the dove type Jezebel—gentle and sweet at first but deadly later. Like a whirlwind, the relationship took off, and she took control of his life. She decided when he came to church and what he did when he came. Even though she was always present and involved, she did not want him always present or involved in anything. If he was given a specific task for a specific service such as opening the Sunday worship service in prayer, she instructed him to stay at home. He complied although he wanted to be in church. The more he was challenged to become involved, the more this woman instructed him to stay at home, even with threats at times. This young man related to the couple leading the church that this Jezebel woman was even physically abusive, but you would never have known it just by looking at her. The couple knew something was wrong with him because he changed from being a pleasant, friendly guy to always looking frazzled and confused. Thus, they tried to build a stronger relationship with him. This woman realized what was happening and instructed this young man to return to his previous church. By this time, her own church attendance had dropped. If this young man disobeyed her instruction and attended services, she called his phone or waited in the parking lot for him. The couple wanted to have a meeting with these two, but the young man was afraid. After she realized that they were on to her, this woman began complaining to the Pastor that this young man was after her to have a relationship. When asked, she was adamant that they never had a relationship. The young man and his siblings and employees claimed otherwise. She always steered clear of the Pastor's wife. She began increasing her complaints against the young man not only to the Pastor but also to other church members. She had a lot of stories and a lot of tears. Her tears won the hearts of people. She was the victim and this young man was the villain. She was embraced while he was marginalized. One of the members suggested that she go to the Pastor's wife with her complaints, but she refused claiming that the Pastor's wife would not show her love.

- **Flattery**. Jezebel loves to flatter. Flattery is usually comparative in nature and appeals to the ego and will draw in those who struggle with their self-esteem. The Holy Spirit never compares one believer against another nor esteem one higher than another.
- **A monitoring spirit.** Jezebels like to be current with all of the plans and activities of their targets. They will use every means necessary to achieve this.
- **Exaggeration**. They do this in every area and on every issue that will cause them to look good.
- **Hypercritical.** They will evaluate and criticize almost everything they did not do or have an input into. They will also criticize those you admire.
- **Has eunuchs in service.** Eunuchs served in the household of kings, in the women's bed chambers. 2 Kings 9:30-32 supports the fact that Queen Jezebel had eunuchs. Eunuchs are castrated males. When the term is used generally, it means an ineffective person. The spirit of Jezebel needs eunuchs to serve her. This spirit will use its eunuch's influence, access, and energy to do its bidding. However, it's interesting to note that it was the eunuchs who threw the wicked Queen Jezebel down. This tells me that God can use eunuchs who are in Jezebel's service against her. "Now when Jehu had come to Jezreel, Jezebel heard *of it;*

and she put paint on her eyes and adorned her head and looked through a window. Then, as Jehu entered at the gate, she said, '*Is it* peace, Zimri, murderer of your master?' And he looked up at the window, and said, 'Who *is* on my side? Who?' So, two *or* three eunuchs looked out at him. Then he said, 'Throw her down.' So they threw her down, and *some* of her blood spattered on the wall and on the horses; and he trampled her underfoot." (2 Kings 9:30-33 NKJV)

- **Female Jezebels have a poor attitude towards men.** The Jezebel spirit holds resentment, hatred, and bitterness towards men based on rejection, abuse, or hurt.
- **Emasculates men.** The Jezebel spirit seeks to emasculate or deprive men of their authority and power. The spirit will foster a distrust and hatred of male authority figures and men in general. When a man has a Jezebel in his life, there is a process in which his masculinity is removed layer by layer. While a male who was raised manly will need to be emasculated, weakened, or castrated, there are some males who were raised soft. Thus it's easy to make them into eunuchs. The goal of emasculating a male is achieved by constantly talking down to him, being hypercritical of him, frequently comparing him with others, micromanaging, or simply taking over his tasks, yelling at him, ignoring, or downplaying his achievements. These are just some of the tactics used. There are too many leaders in the Body of Christ who are unable to be the blessing they were ordained to be because they are controlled by women who conjure emotions and biases only indigenous to women.

Reflection

1. Am I using free will to erect idols in my life?
2. Is my will continuously surrendered to the authority of the Holy Spirit?

Prayer and Declaration

Father, I surrender my heart to you. Purify my heart, O God. I desire to live a pure, holy life. I want to be free of rebellion and every other trait that offends You. Proverbs 4:23 admonishes me to keep my heart with all diligence, for out of it spring the issues of life. Grant me the grace to please You at all times, in Jesus' name. Amen.

Chapter 3:

Ahab: A Match Made in Demonic Heaven

King Ahab married Jezebel, the Phoenician Princess. This marriage elevated Jezebel from a princess to a queen. Her status as queen empowered her to exercise control over God's people. Jezebel and Ahab had quite a bit in common.

Like Jezebel, Ahab also sprang from an idolatrous root. Here is how God appraised Ahab's father kingship: "Omri did evil in the eyes of the Lord and did worse than all who *were* before him. For he walked in all the ways of Jeroboam the son of Nebat, and in his sin by which he had made Israel sin, provoking the Lord God of Israel to anger with their idols'" (1 Kings 16:25–26 NKJV). What were the ways of Jeroboam? Baal worship! "Therefore, the king asked advice, made two calves of gold, and said to the people, 'It is too much for you to go up to Jerusalem. Here are your gods, O Israel, which brought you up from the land of Egypt!' (1 Kings 12:28 NKJV) Wherever a bull or an image of a bull is worshipped, Baal is worshipped.

1 Samuel 15:23 says, "For rebellion is as the sin of witchcraft and stubbornness is as iniquity and idolatry…." (NKJV) Jezebel did not start anything new. The foundations for Baal worship had already been laid by the kings of Israel. The Scripture compares rebellion to witchcraft. Both rebellion and witchcraft spring from the single soulish DNA of self-will. Thus, they are evil twins; wherever one is, the other will eventually show up. Anytime an individual is rebel-

lious for long enough, they will begin to manifest witchcraft traits. Merriam Webster's Dictionary defines "rebellion" as *opposition to one in authority or dominance.* Open, armed, and usually unsuccessful defiance of or resistance to an established government; an instance of such defiance or resistance." Rebellion is not always a bold renegade; sometimes it's a great idea. However, good intentions or great ideas do not make it right to divert from that which has been laid out by authority figures or the written Word of God.

Ahab built on the foundation of idolatry and rebellion his father had laid. "Now Ahab the son of Omri did evil in the sight of the Lord, more than all who *were* before him. And it came to pass, as though it had been a trivial thing for him to walk in the sins of Jeroboam the son of Nebat, that he took as wife Jezebel the daughter of Ethbaal, king of the Sidonians; and he went and served Baal and worshiped him." (1 Kings 16:30-31 NKJV)

Ahab and Jezebel both had the same spiritual DNA; thus, they were a perfect match. Every Jezebel needs an Ahab, and every Ahab needs a Jezebel. It's a co-dependent, highly functional demonic team. So, why was God angry because Ahab married Jezebel? Besides her being a heathen princess, it was believed that Jezebel was a priestess of Baal, thus she had the knowledge of and the passion for establishing Baal worship in a greater way in Israel. Her defiance against Yahweh manifested itself as witchcraft when she laid her will and way of worship on God's people even to the point that she persecuted and killed His prophets.

Ahab is often portrayed as a weak individual, but I will differ. Ahab was a king and a military leader. He was simply evil. His marriage to Jezebel cemented his journey down the evil path. God had already warned his people concerning marrying heathen women: "Nor shall you make marriages with them. You shall not give your daughter to their son, nor take their daughter for your son. For they will turn your sons away from following Me, to serve other gods; so the anger of the Lord will be aroused against you and destroy you suddenly."

(Deuteronomy 7:3-4 NKJV) Whenever we are dealing with evil, the individual with the greater devotion always rises to the top. This is what happened with Ahab and Jezebel. They both worshipped Baal. It's just that she had a greater passion for establishing the worship of this deity than Ahab did, thus Ahab let her be.

A Few Personality Traits of People with an Ahab Spirit

Before I continue, let's be conscious of the fact that, like the spirit of Jezebel, Ahab is also a spirit; thus, gender-neutral. Therefore, a male or a female can be influenced by this spirit. It's also important to always remember that individuals in an Ahab-Jezebel relationship always have common ground, even though the Ahab may act like a victim. If you are trying to take an Ahab through deliverance, you may need to excavate their past and current relationship and interactions with the Jezebelic personality. The common ground could be soul ties, family ties, shared secrets that Ahab does not want revealed, some form of indebtedness, or so on. The common ground may take time to uncover or be discovered easily through discernment or a word of knowledge. It also depends on the honesty of the Ahab personality.

Traits:

- Quickly and conveniently relinquish power.
- Compensate for their low self-esteem by being nice and likeable.
- Overly concerned about the opinion of others.
- Think it's their role to make everyone happy.
- Tend to be clingy.
- Struggle to accept God's ability to change their situation.
- Struggle to walk in their God-given freedom.
- Will often go deeper into Jezebel's bondage instead of walking away.
- Overlook too many faults in people's personalities.
- Fear conflict.
- Avoid being assertive.

- Fear rejection.
- Tolerate evil.
- Pretentious and projects the image of being moral and upright but indulges in secret sin.
- They are attracted to domineering personalities of the opposite sex.
- A female with an Ahab spirit will magnetize to and regularly find themselves in friendships with females who have a Jezebel spirit.

Bewitched

Many times, Ahabs are under a Jezebel's spell. When an individual is spellbound by someone, they are fascinated or controlled to the point that they cannot think or function without that person's input. Such persons tend to avoid confrontation even to their detriment. They will avoid confrontation at any cost, mainly because they feel intimidated by the consequences of confronting Jezebel. Thus, they prefer to suffer or allow others to suffer. While it's always wise to maintain a peaceful environment, it's not real peace if the sense of tranquility does not benefit all involved.

The Holy Spirit showed me that there are leaders operating in an Ahab spirit, thus allowing Jezebel to rule and ravish God's people because they don't want to have to deal with the consequences and discomfort of confrontation. Thus, they make excuses for or ignore those with Jezebelic personalities.

Ahabs Allow Jezebels to Do Their Dirty Work

"And it came to pass after these things that Naboth the Jezreelite had a vineyard which was in Jezreel, next to the palace of Ahab king of Samaria. So, Ahab spoke to Naboth, saying, 'Give me your vineyard that I may have it for a vegetable garden, because it is near, next to my house; and for it I will give you a vineyard better than it. Or, if it seems good to you, I will give you its worth in money.' But Naboth said to Ahab, 'The Lord forbid that I should give the inheritance of my fathers to you!' So Ahab went into his house sullen and displeased because of the word which Naboth the Jezreelite had spoken to him; for he had said, 'I will not give you the inheritance of my fathers.' And he lay down on his bed, and turned away his face, and would eat no food. But Jezebel his wife came to him, and said to him, 'Why is your spirit so sullen that you eat no food?' He said to her, 'Because I spoke to Naboth the Jezreelite, and said to him, "Give me your vineyard for money; or else, if it pleases you, I will give you another vineyard for it." And he answered, "I will not give you my vineyard."' Then Jezebel his wife said to him, 'You now exercise authority over Israel! Arise, eat food, and let your heart be cheerful; I will give you the vineyard of Naboth the Jezreelite.' (1 Kings 21:1-7 NKJV)

When Ahab cannot have your inheritance, your substance or your servitude; when you refuse to surrender your destiny, your time, and your talent to him, he will release Jezebel on you like a wild Pit Bull while he plays the victim, fully aware of the consequences of his actions. King Ahab knew the personality of his wife. He knew she would go after Naboth's vineyard on his behalf and he conveniently relinquished authority for this purpose. Every Ahab knows the personality of those around them. They know who they can conveniently release information to so that that person or persons come after you.

Jezebel Hates the True Prophetic

"For so it was, while Jezebel massacred the prophets of the Lord, that Obadiah had taken one hundred prophets and hidden them, fifty to a cave, and had fed them with bread and water." (1 Kings 18:4 NKJV)

In Chapter 2, I established that Jezebel has a prophetic voice. Therefore, I do not believe this spirit hates the prophetic. It just hates the *true* prophetic. Jezebel hates and sets out to destroy true prophets. It will seek to attach itself to prophets of the Lord or infiltrate prophetic circles and ministries with the end goal of controlling, contaminating, or destroying. Apostles, by nature, are very prophetic. Hence, they will often come under strong attack from this spirit. Some apostles and prophets may experience more intense and frequent attacks from this spirit than others.

Why Jezebel hates true prophets and prophetic people:

- True prophets focus on and accurately discern motives.
- They focus on the intent on the heart.
- They discern and hate falsehood and deception.
- Prophets see what other five-folders don't see.
- They will discern and resist any form of control.
- Hate flattery and slander.
- Will resist any form of perversion.
- True prophets will address the issue of the elephant in the room. They deal with issues others prefer to sweep under the rug. They will say what others are afraid to say and ask questions others are afraid to ask.
- Prophets are God-focused. They are surrendered to the will of God.
- They will identify, confront, and expose Jezebel and her false prophets.

What Triggers a Witchcraft Attack?

Spiritual Victory: I remembered years ago when I was one of the lead worshippers in the church I attended back then. Whenever I led worship—whether it was Sunday morning or evening, and there was a strong release of the Spirit of God—in a matter of hours or days, I would come under intense attacks of lies, slanders, and accusations. At that time, I did not know it was witchcraft, but it had become a predictable pattern.

The prophet Elijah suffered mental attacks after he killed Jezebel's prophets. "And Ahab told Jezebel all that Elijah had done, also how he had executed all the prophets with the sword. Then Jezebel sent a messenger to Elijah, saying, 'So let the gods do *to me,* and more also, if I do not make your life as the life of one of them by tomorrow about this time.' And when he saw *that,* he arose and ran for his life, and went to Beersheba, which *belongs* to Judah, and left his servant there." (1 Kings 19:1-3)

Seasons of Transition: Whenever God is about to transition or promote a prophet or prophetic person, there are often heightened witchcraft attacks.

Seasons of Birthing: When that which God has placed in the prophet's spirit is about to be birthed, or an assignment realized, there may be heightened witchcraft activities.

Confrontation with Jezebel: It takes courage to confront Jezebel. Confrontation will lead to exposure. This spirit and its personalities hate exposure. When they are exposed, they will come at you with false prophetic utterances, cursing, and everything else they have got.

Signs That You Are Under the Attack of Witchcraft

If you are experiencing one or two signs from this list, it does not mean you are under the attack of witchcraft. It could simply mean that you are experiencing some of the challenges that come with life. When someone is under the attack of witchcraft, several of these signs will manifest either together or in rapid succession.

- **Onslaught of lies**: Satan is a liar, and so is his offspring Jezebel. Lies can come from any direction: people you know, people you have very little interaction with, or people you don't know at all. However, the enemy will always try to use someone seemingly credible to lie against you. In that way, the hearers will not question what they hear because of its source.
- **Slander and accusations:** Satan is sometimes described as "Slanderer" or "False Accuser." Slander and accusations are weapons in Jezebel's arsenal. "And she wrote letters in Ahab's name, sealed *them* with his seal, and sent the letters to the elders

and the nobles who *were* dwelling in the city with Naboth. She wrote in the letters, saying, 'Proclaim a fast, and seat Naboth with high honor among the people; and seat two men, scoundrels, before him to bear witness against him, saying, "You have blasphemed God and the king." *Then* take him out, and stone him, that he may die.'" (1 Kings 21:8-10)

- **Curses:** Jezebel is a witch. Witches pronounce curses. This demon will influence others to speak negative words, destruction, and even death to you and everything you are associated with or connected to.
- **Witchcraft prayers:** People who utter this type of prayer prey on the will and desires of others. Such prayers are intended to manipulate or influence people's decisions and directions. This too can be a type of curse since it can create hindrances and challenges for the individual whom such utterances are made about. Romans 2:4 tells us that the goodness of God leads to repentance. God wants people to come to Him out of their own free will because of His goodness. Further, John 16:8 tells us, "And when He has come, He will convict the world of sin, and of righteousness, and of judgment." The Holy Spirit is the one who draws people to Christ, not disaster.

If we want God to answer our prayers, then we must pray the Word of God and the will of God in situations. How do we know the will of God? From His written word, via prophetic utterances and by the leading of the Holy Spirit.

- **False prophetic utterances:** A true prophetic vessel can give a false prophetic utterance. A false prophetic utterance is saying what God did not say or editing and adjusting what God said. No one can accidentally do this. It's usually done deliberately for selfish reasons. This type of behavior removes the integrity and credibility from the prophetic vessel. If you are going to speak on behalf of God, always value and maintain integrity in your utterances. Whenever you discern false prophetic utterances, cancel the same in the name of Jesus and declare God's word and promises over your life. Such utterances can become a curse

since it can create hindrances and unnecessary struggles in your life.
- **Imaginations:** This type of attack targets the internal, visual aspect of your personality. The aim is to twist it and cause it to function according to a demonic intent. Thus, when you are under this type of attack, negative and demonic originated thoughts and imaginations will bombard your mind that will cause you to either retreat or surrender to control. It brings with it fear, doubt, confusion, and intimidation. It can cause you to overthink things or behave in a paranoid manner. Elijah retreated to a cave after Jezebel threatened his life because he already had visuals of what she had done with other prophets.
- **Provocation**: This includes jeering, teasing, mocking, and name-calling.
- **Confusion**: When confusion sets in, you will question relationships, your calling, and even your faith.
- **Forgetfulness**: You forget easily and make simple mistakes. You may go to a place and wonder why you are there when you get there.
- **Sickness**: When you are under the attack of witchcraft, you may feel sick and have headaches and pains that you do not otherwise have.
- **Weariness**: The enemy will try to wear you down physically, mentally, and emotionally with assaults so that you give into the spirit of control. The enemy also comes after your support system—those who are standing with you to make them weary with your battles and abandon you. Weariness can also result in your dropping projects you were excited about.
- **Sleepiness or sleeplessness:** Some people struggle with sleepiness or sleeplessness during these times. The sleeping patterns go against their normal flow.
- **Desire to quit**: You will want to give up on things you were passionate about and even relationships that are meaningful.
- **Loss of identity:** Depending on the intensity of the attack, you may forget who you are and the authority you have in Christ.
- **Desire to isolate**: During this time, the desire is there to cut

people off or avoid interaction. Getting into your cave and being alone seems to be a wiser choice. This is one of the main goals of the spirit of witchcraft—to isolate you.
- **Depression:** The assaults from this spirit cause you to sink into a state of despair and hopelessness. The prophet Elijah became depressed while under witchcraft attack. "But he himself went a day's journey into the wilderness and came and sat down under a broom tree. And he prayed that he might die, and said, 'It is enough! Now, Lord, take my life, for I *am* no better than my fathers!'" (1 King 19:4)
- **Self-destructive behavior:** Depression can morph and produce self-destructive tendencies and residual habits. This can manifest in two ways, one being where you want to harm yourself. Sometimes, it just happens in a short space of time, without your giving it much thought; other times, it sort of flows out of depression. It's always wise to reach out for help if this type of thought pattern persists.

The second way in which this manifests is in self-sabotaging behaviors. This is where you develop habits that ruin relationships. Sometimes, it's not done consciously; and sometimes, it's done out of fear. Let's remember that habits are developed; therefore, they can be changed by firstly acknowledging that you have been wounded and are hurting. Secondly, seeking healing in your emotions and thirdly developing strategies necessary for mutually beneficial and long-lasting relationships.
- **Feeling of fear:** Fear keeps you in a place of constant torment and lack of confidence in God's promises and His Word.
- **Headache and dizziness:** This may differ from person to person. For me, when I am under an intense witchcraft attack, I have headaches and dizziness during unusual times. The dizziness shows up, particularly while driving.

Reflection

1. Have I thoroughly removed every demonic root in my life?
2. Do I regularly find myself magnetized to Jezebelic personalities?
3. Am I conscious of seasons in which Jezebel's attacks against me are intensified?
4. Now that I understand that rebellion can be a subtle attitude of the heart, how do I guard my heart to ensure I am not rebellious towards God and godly authority?

Prayer and Declaration

I stand in the authority of the name of Jesus Christ and I uproot every demonic seed planted in my life through rejection, abandonment, abuse, fear, lust, lies, slander and accusations, word curses, witchcraft prayers, false prophetic utterance, and every other demonic deposit. I curse every seed of the enemy and I command them to wither and die. I decree that according to Isaiah 61:3, I am a tree of righteousness, the planting of the Lord. I decree, I am fruitful and favored in Jesus' name. Amen.

Chapter 4:

Weapons and Tactics of Jezebel

As we look at the weapons and tactics of Jezebel, let us remember that Ephesians 6:12 says, "For we do not wrestle against flesh and blood, but against principalities, against powers, against the rulers of the darkness of this age, against spiritual *hosts* of wickedness in the heavenly *places.*" In the previous chapters, I've established that the spirit of Jezebel works witchcraft against its victim. The purpose of witchcraft is to bring its victim firmly under the control of this entity or individual through whom this entity functions. Let us also remember that in most instances, the manifestations of witchcraft are often perceived and "passed off" as the personality of an individual because this entity functions through the carnal and the natural nature of human beings.

Jezebel's Favorite Strategies of Control

Manipulation

The purpose of manipulation is to pressure a victim into submission through:

Silence or ignoring: This happens if a person dares to disagree with, refuses to comply with, or does not allow a Jezebelic person to have their way.

Tantrums: These are outbursts of anger or frustration intended to cause the victim to give in.

Tears: Tears are intended to project innocence and win empathy.

Flattery: This is insincere praise. It's usually given with an ulterior motive. Flattery is comparative in nature. The Holy Spirit will never compare one believer to another. He will not inspire a word of prophecy that He has blessed or will bless, anoint, or use one individual more than another. Always recognize this type of behavior as witchcraft. It appeals to the ego and causes the victim to begin to function out of the carnal nature. Flattery is not a compliment. Compliments are genuine and polite expression of praise and admiration. Compliments are not comparative nor carnally flavored.

Prophecy: Jezebel will give you flattering prophecies to navigate you away from godly leadership and its influence when it discerns that you are feeling rejected or overlooked. Jezebel will also release false prophecies when it recognizes that you are seeking to move from under its control.

Emotional outbursts: These are different from tantrums. The emotions conjured serve the purpose of making a lie or a fabricated incident sound genuine. Once, I was in a meeting with a group of Christian leaders. The leader of this group was convening the meeting and lying about a particular incident up for discussion. This is the kind of person that, when engaging them in conversation, you need to hook them up to a lie detector if you don't have discernment. At this meeting, no one was judging this man of God based on his habit. Everyone in the group knew he was lying about this particular incident. However, no one told him he was lying. In fact, no one engaged him in any way. Instead, everyone quietly listened. Apparently, our silence echoed our disbelief. So, this man took things to the next level. He dropped to his knees, erupted into tears, and continued lying.

Anger: This strategy is intended to challenge and cause an individual to rethink their position on a matter due to yelling, stomping their feet, slamming doors, swearing, and so on.

Show of remorse or repentance: It requires discernment to detect the insincerity when someone does this, since it's usually accompanied by all of the right words and emotions. This tactic is intended to neutralize any resistance and win over all opposition.

Gifts: Not everyone who give gifts is a Jezebel. Some people are simply generous or kind. However, Jezebels love to give gifts, but Jezebel's gifts have an agenda. They want to win the recipient's favor, cause the recipient to feel obligated to act in their favor in the present or future, and be indebted to their cause whenever it may arise.

The guardian of information: Jezebel likes to give the impression that they have information no one else has. If they give information, they tend to do so in portions. They will tell you something but seemingly withhold a critical or connecting part of the conversation. In that way, you will chase after them to find out more. In many cases, they aren't holding anything significant, or they have nothing at all.

They may tell you God told them something or showed them something. I know of someone who had a Jezebel attending their ministry. After creating some confusion and undermining leadership, this woman was asked to leave. She left, cursing the ministry on the way out, and claimed that God showed her what would happen to the ministry. Interestingly, this woman didn't have a history of being prophetic or hearing from God. She, however, conveniently heard from God on her way out. Out of sheer curiosity, one of the leaders reached out and enquired what God had shown her. Her response was, "You will see!"

They also like to store information shared during the good times and information shared in confidence so that they can use it against you later. Sometimes, the Holy Spirit will caution you when you're about to share certain types of information with some people. Never ignore that cautioning. Jezebels are also known for secretly recording conversations.

Removing access or privileges: This is one of the consequences of not complying or agreeing on certain matters with a Jezebel or outright refusing to be manipulated. They will remove you from teams, positions and their inner circle. Any privileges you enjoyed will be revoked and promises made to you will be cancelled.

A Jezebelic type of covering leader will remove levels of access or privilege from a member of his or her network or completely remove covering.

Shifting position: This strategy is specifically used as it relates to upward mobility, whether in ministry or otherwise, and is used by a superior against a subordinate. Jezebels will validate their reason for sidelining or not promoting you, claiming that you are not competent or capable of functioning in the required capacity, completely ignoring the fact that they previously endorsed and proclaimed you the most proficient and suitable for elevation. This can become a physiological battle because they will relate this misrepresentation to their superiors or peers if you contest their decision to elevate someone else instead of you. Those who don't know you in contested capacity will believe their report. I believe this is one of the classic moves of a witchcraft spirit.

Confusing a conversation: This happens mainly during confrontation. They try to take control of the conversation by constantly changing its direction. It's difficult to pin them down on a specific line of discussion. If they realize they cannot control the conversation, they will accuse you of not giving them a fair chance to speak.

Intimidation

This is another tactic used by someone with a witchcraft spirit. This is done through:

Threats: This serves the purpose of maintaining control over a victim. A Jezebel will threaten to have a non-compliant individual removed and replaced from a position or place. Jezebels are also known to have threatened to commit suicide. In a marriage, they can threaten to file for divorce.

Shouting and yelling: When a superior on a job or a leader in a ministry shouts and yells at another individual, especially an adult and especially if it's done frequently or in the presence of others, intimidation and shaming is the main intent.

Character assassination: Accusations, slander, and lies are all strategies used by Jezebel to discredit and destroy its target. I've had a lengthy season of dealing with accusations, slander, and lies from Jezebelic people. This season of attack was particularly frustrating for me because one thing popped up right after another. The moment I thought one situation had died or had been dealt with, another popped up. This type of attack can cause you to feel overwhelmed, especially if you are in an environment in which people are unable to discern it's an attack.

The enemy is relentless and will always find someone to use. The enemy is also strategic; thus, seemingly credible people will be used in this attack. The spirit of witchcraft can sit on anyone and influence them against you. Remember, it functions through the carnal or natural nature of a person. All the enemy needs is someone with unhealthy emotions towards you such as hate, resentment, envy, insecurity, or the like and they can be influenced and used. Many times, people are unaware that they are under the influence of a spirit of witchcraft.

Character assassination has destiny-killing demons assigned to it. Attacks of accusation, slander, and lies are assigned to push you into a cave and bury you there even before you recognize who you are or what God has called you to do. The enemy can also take this to another level by causing his agents to gang up on or play tag team against you. I will explain this strategy later in this chapter.

Domination

When someone is being dominated, their power to agree, disagree, or make decisions is removed. Man was created to walk in dominion. Then God said, "Let Us make man in Our image, according to Our likeness; let them have dominion over the fish of the sea, over the birds of the air, and over the cattle, over all the earth and over every creeping thing that creeps on the earth." (Genesis 1:26)

Since the fall of man in the Garden of Eden, we see man seeking to have dominion over man. This is so because man was created to have dominion. When man fell, his nature became corrupt. Therefore, he no longer walks in dominion according to design but according to his corrupt desires. Man should have dominion over creation, not over one another.

In a friendship or among acquaintances when one individual is seeking to have dominion over you, they will illegitimately assume the superior role in the relationship. They may even be bold enough to enter the relationship giving instructions, directions, corrections, and rebuke. They will always find ways to take the lead or be in charge. This ought not to be so. In a friendship or amongst acquaintances, everyone is on the same level, unless it has been situationally or unanimously agreed upon to recognize a leader.

There may be instances in which you may be in or seeking to build a relationship with someone more senior than you in ministry. This, however, does not make them leader over you or gives them the right to assume seniority in the relationship. Unless they are the leader of the ministry you attend or the leader of a team that you are a part of. However, if they hold no form of seniority over you in ministry or work environment, they have no right to assume seniority in the relationship. I am in no way implying that the appropriate honor should be removed. I believe in a culture of honor and encourage everyone to give honor to whom it is due. However, there needs to be clarity in this area because there are too many ministers of the gospel who don't know how to build a relationship without trying to boss others around. They think they are senior in every environment. Thus, they try to correct, direct, instruct, and rebuke people who are not under their leadership. This type of behavior is Jezebelic. Only the spiritual leadership of an individual or ministry holds the right to correct, instruct, direct, or rebuke. If it's a leadership team, this protocol has to be done according to the guidelines set out by the team. Coaches and mentors also hold this right. Anyone outside the aforementioned has no right, as senior, influential, or anointed as they may be. All must understand that certain privileges are not automatic; rather, they are granted through having the appropriate relationship.

With that being said, here are a few other signs that you are being dominated:

- If you are a part of a team or sub-ministry in your church, but you are not free to give input.
- If you are not free to find expression in your area of gifting or passion. I once heard a story of a young lady who was the lead worshipper in her church. She was very anointed and led the worship well, but her passion was dancing. She loved to dance; this she did excellently also. Every time this young lady told her pastor that she wanted to dance, he would tell her, "No, I don't want you dancing. I want you to focus on leading worship." This repeatedly happened until this young lady became frustrated and gave up her passion. There is a difference between leading and dominating. This young lady could have been allowed to flow in both areas.
- If you are assigned a task and then the person who gave you the task tells you how to do it, not allowing you to use your thoughts or creativity.
- Being micro-managed is also a sign of domination.

With that being said, the structures and protocols a church or leader has in place must be respected; and as such, should not be considered control.

Word curses: Sickness, death, destruction, delayed or aborted destiny, estrangement in relationships, and struggles in ministry are just a few of the things that can result from word curses. There is no witchcraft without curses. The Lexicon Dictionary describes a "curse" as *A solemn utterance intended to invoke a supernatural power to inflict harm or punishment on someone or something. Synonyms: malediction, hex, jinx.*

Riding on this definition, let's see what the Bible has to say about words and curses. Proverbs 18:21 says, "Death and life *are* in the power of the tongue, and those who love it will eat its fruit." (NKJV) Thus, every time we speak, we are releasing either life or death to whatever we are speaking about. Consequently, whether we are conscious of this or not, when we speak, we are invoking supernatural powers. We are sending angels or demons into action.

Those who function out of witchcraft will relentlessly release curses on their targets, fully conscious of their intent which is harm, destruction, and death. James 3:8-10 is a clear description of such a person: "But no man can tame the tongue. *It is* an unruly evil, full of deadly poison. With it we bless our God and Father, and with it we curse men, who have been made in the similitude of God. Out of the same mouth proceed blessing and cursing. My brethren, these things ought not to be so." (NKJV) Blessing and cursing proceeding from the same place is a sign of contaminated heart. The fact that no man can tame the tongue is no excuse. We have the Holy Spirit to help us. Word curses are a manifestation of a witchcraft spirit, regardless of how titled in the fivefold or otherwise the one who practice this type of behavior is. The Scriptures never authorized us to release word curses on anyone. Even if someone has offended us, we should allow God to vindicate us rather than slip into witchcraft. Witches pronounce curses. Sometimes, we need to step back and examine our hearts before we speak. Are you a witch or a servant of the Most High God? Are your words testifying of your answer?

On many occasions, I've witnessed leaders release word curses, hexes, and spells on members whenever they leave their ministry or covering. Also, based on the definition, we understand that curses are utterances or spoken words. I used the phrase "word curses" for clarity's sake since there are other types of curses. In my opinion, a member leaving is one of the greatest tests of a leader's maturity. Very rarely will you find a leader who will acknowledge that seasons change or that people need to move on in their destiny and release them with a pure heart. Many take things personally and slip into a fit of word cursing. It's witchcraft.

We should never take a light approach to word curses. We should never ignore word curses. Word curses cannot be overcome by will power. Words create things. Negative words spoken over you will become negative things manifesting in your life. I had a poor approach to word curses. I always thought that I could overcome word curses by will power, especially if the curses go against my character. I would brush them aside, thinking, "That's not who I am, or that's not something I am inclined to do," only to later develop a struggle that sometimes becomes full blown warfare in that specific area. People may speak accusations based on suspicion or a lie. Never leave those words hanging over your life, especially if the same thing is said repeatedly by those in authority over you. Remember, whatever you allow is allowed, whatever you disallow is disallowed. (See Matthew 18:18.) Word curses are broken or cancelled in the name of Jesus.

Often, believers leave word curses hanging over their lives because they misunderstand this Scripture, "Christ has redeemed us from the curse of the law, having become a curse for us for it is written, 'Cursed *is* everyone who hangs on a tree.'" (Galatians 3:13) This Scripture is referring to the curse of the law; not word curses or curses or witchcraft. The law brought a curse on humanity, but Jesus Christ delivered the redeemed from that curse.

On the other hand, don't become too obsessed with word curses. Proverbs 26:2 says, "Like a flitting sparrow, like a flying swallow, So a curse without cause shall not alight." Word curses from certain people and in certain situations will have no weight over your life. This, however, is not a license to be careless.

Word curses produce heaviness over your life. There are times, the Holy Spirit—via the gift of Word of Knowledge or Discernment of Spirits—will cause you to hear people releasing word curses over you as an individual, over your family, or ministry. And there are times you will become aware via other means.

Hebrews 13:3 tells us, "By faith we understand that the worlds were framed by the Word of God, so that the things which are seen were not made of things which are visible." This Scripture speaks of creation, the physical world that God spoke into existence; but as it is in the natural, so it is in the spiritual. I believe that before you were born into this world, God already spoke your world, His desires for you, the reason He sent you to earth, your destiny into existence; and at the appointed time as you follow the leadings of the Holy Spirit, you will come into alignment to fulfill your destiny. This is why receiving prophetic ministry is important, because it helps you understand what your life should look like.

However, Satan tries to rewrite destinies with word curses! This is why you should never leave word curses hanging over your life. Rather, come into agreement with God. Declare God's written and prophetic words over your life. Whenever God speaks to you prophetically, make those prophetic words into declarations and frame your world; speak them into existence. By doing this, you come into agreement with your Heavenly Father, thus vanquishing Satan's utterances.

Demon Gangs

Gangs are self-organized groups of people bonded by a sense of loyalty, family, and similar goals. They usually:

- Are not legally sanctioned or supported.
- Claim control over a territory.
- Support one another. Gang members are required to support or back one another up, whether it's in committing a crime or protection against an enemy. No one has to pass down instructions for support of a member. It's simply an unwritten rule.
- Highly organized gangs have a clearly defined leadership and code of operation.
- Demon gangs work similarly. I used the word "gang" in relation to the teamwork of demons because, in many ways, they resemble a gang.
- They have no legal authority to function in the earth realm except with the permission of man.
- They claim or seek to claim control over a territory. This could be an individual, family, community, business, church, company, nation, or region.
- They are highly organized. Demons work in teams. Even though at first, it may seem as though an individual is battling one demon; in most cases, there are more lurking in the background ready to give support to the attack or are already working behind the scenes. Further, on every level and assignment, there is teamwork. For example, the spirit of Jezebel can team up with a religious spirit, the spirit of Athilah—a spirit that resembles Jezebel but is lesser in power and influence, the spirit of python, the spirit of Absalom, the spirit of abuse, Leviathan, and so on. However, these are all strongmen, like the leaders of highly organized gangs. The aforementioned are more involved in strategizing and conducting major transactions. They don't do lower level work.

Lower level demons could be lie, anger, jealousy, and hate; but they work together and back up each other; and most of all, they

Exposing Jezebel

work to keep the strong man undetected. Thus, without Holy Spirit discernment or knowledge of the workings and manifestations of the strongman, it could take a while to figure out what you are dealing with because the lower level demons keep you engaged and distracted. Lack of knowledge or discernment in this area can cause you to go in circles for a long time.

Tag Teams

People with the spirit of witchcraft tag each other. Someone with the spirit of witchcraft in your family can tag someone in your church or someone on your job can tag someone in your church by passing on a lie or scandal so that your torment continues when you are out of their reach.

This can also happen if a member leaves one witchcraft church environment to attend another church. There are occasions in which leaders may meet to discuss the transitioning of the member. When the leaders meet, the witchcraft leader giving a negative or false report can influence the new leader to continue the mistreatment of that individual. If the new leader already has witchcraft tendencies, then it becomes easy to get tagged. It's a spiritual transfer. For this reason, it's not only fair but beneficial for that member if they are invited to be a part of such a meeting.

Also, demons from one geographic location can tag demons in the new geographic location when someone under attack relocates. This transfer is done in the realm of the spirit, and the demon in the new location is then tasked with finding a suitable human agent to use against the target...

Siege

"Siege" is defined by the Free Online Dictionary as *the offensive operations carried out to capture a fortified place by surrounding it, severing its communications and supply lines, and deploying weapons against it. A persistent attempt to gain something.*

A witchcraft siege is a coordinated attack that can come from:

- **Internal source:** There are times your mind comes under heavy and consistent bombardment of demonic whispers which can produce unhealthy thought patterns that causes you to feel deflated, defeated, and ready to walk away from your destiny. During these times, it's unwise to isolate yourself because the enemy can use the opportunity to draw you into a place of depression. Rather, these are the times you may need to reach out to your confidants or prayer partners. During these times, it's critical that you spend time in prayer even though it may feel as though your prayer is not going to pass the ceiling—push pass that feeling and keep pressing in prayer.
- **External sources:** This can manifest in being consistently ganged up on or plotted against.
- **Persistent attacks:** When an individual has been under attack for a prolonged period, it's a siege.

Guerrilla Warfare

The use of hit-and-run tactics. It's attacking from a distance or safe place. The goal is to harass or sabotage. Preaching rumors, hearsay, and scandal is guerrilla warfare. It's a strategy used by people who are not bold enough to comfort and converse on a one-on-one basis.

Infiltration

When you discern and disconnect from a Jezebelic personality, they will find ways to infiltrate your circle of friends or family so that they may continue to monitor and manipulate you via others. Suddenly, you will observe that Jezebel is trying to befriend and connect with those close to you. Many times, these people are unsuspecting and undiscerning that they are simply channels through which Jezebel wants to keep current with your plans and activities. Jezebel will also use these connections to question your choices and decisions and even present their way as a better option. For this reason, you need to avoid confiding in or revealing your plans to those in your circle who are obviously desperate for status, acceptance, or have a history of being disloyal. Remember, in most cases, Jezebel holds a level of influence and can easily win the aforementioned type of people with flattery, promises, or presents.

Reflection

1. Do I allow others to dominate me? If yes, what steps should I take to change that?
2. Do I seek to exercise illegitimate authority in the life of those around me? If yes, what steps should I take to change that?
3. Do I have any trait of Jezebel in my life?

Prayer and Declaration

Father, in the name of Jesus, I disarm and dethrone every Jezebel assigned to my life. I relieve them of every weapon and every strategy designed for my loved ones and me. I declare we are hidden from every monitoring spirit. I block the path of every person assigned to monitor my family and I, and I block the path of every other agent of Jezebel. I declare they have no access to my loved ones or me. Father, I pray that you insert into my circle godly relationships and connections, in Jesus' name. Amen.

Chapter 5:

Witchcraft in the Church

The church is one of the most influential places in society. To the believer, it's home away from home; for many, it's the place they escape to and the place that gives them a sense of belonging. Unfortunately, it's one of the places in which witchcraft is rampant, undetected, thus, unconfronted. A witchcraft church environment will result in God's people living under bondage instead of enjoying the liberty Christ died to give.

Witchcraft in the church can come from both leadership and membership. In my approach to highlighting and bringing education regarding witchcraft in the church, I will firstly focus on witchcraft from leadership. Before I proceed, I would like to make it clear that I believe in and highly value leadership. I believe Christian leadership is critical, not only to church members but to the wider society as a whole. The task of leading people can be challenging and sometimes seemingly unrewarding. I also believe that members should honor and submit to godly leadership as stated in Hebrews 13:17: "Obey them that have the rule over you and submit yourselves: for they watch for your souls, as they that must give account, that they may do it with joy, and not with grief: for that is unprofitable for you."

However, the fact cannot be ignored that some leaders have stepped away from being led by the Spirit of God and began functioning out of witchcraft. Leaders, like any other individual who function out of the spirit of witchcraft, can do so knowingly or unknowingly. Leaders who function out of witchcraft controls God's people instead of leading them. Below I will list traits of a witchcraft-type leader. If you find yourself in this category, please bear in mind that the information is for correction and not condemnation.

Traits of a Witchcraft Leader

In ministry, these leaders tend to use guerilla warfare tactics. They will often preach gossip and hearsay, attacking people from the pulpit. They like to rebuke and correct publicly, intimidating people into submission. At times, they strategically mention people's past, using it against them. These leaders give affirmation sparingly, and love "yes" people who always agree with them. They will not usually elevate free-thinkers to positions of authority within the church, for fear of being challenged. In fact, they discourage free will, calling those who question their theology "rebellious" and "unsubmissive." They view opposing opinions and positions on a matter as personal rejection. These leaders are often not versatile when interpreting the Scripture, and sometimes teach and even enforce erroneous doctrine, claiming to be the only one who has revelation on certain doctrinal truth.

Such leaders show little or no compassion or emotion, viewing them as weakness. They struggle to admit when they're wrong and won't rectify the situation, often lying and misrepresenting those involved in order to validate their own actions.

Leaders like this do not produce true disciples. They tend to curse those who choose to leave and discourage members who choose to stay from having a relationship with the ones who left. An interesting new trend is that these people are often social media stalkers. They discourage members from pursuing a higher education, perhaps relying on ignorance to keep them under control. They even try to control members' attire and appearance, saying that certain things are "immodest" or unacceptable in Christian circles.

These leaders seem to flourish in an atmosphere of strife, creating division and suspicion amongst members. If a leader like this is female, she may surround herself with little Jezebels or Athilahs. Athilah was the name of the daughter of Jezebel and Ahab. Even though Jezebelic personalities produce Athilahs, they will distance themselves from these individuals in times of confrontation.

Jezebelic leaders tend to use prophecy as a means of control and manipulation, leaving members in a situation where they feel that they are disobeying God if they do not submit to the supposed "prophecy."

Regarding the family life of members, these leaders are many times invasive of their personal lives, not paying much attention to the usual boundaries such as appropriate times to call. They like to invade and control family life, turning married couples against each other. I've witnessed controlling leaders on several occasions, making attempts that were often successful in bringing strife and separation to marriages, especially in situations in which this leader is unable to exercise total control over the marriage or if one spouse is prophetic. I've known of male leaders with a witchcraft spirit targeting and trifling with the wives of their leaders, specifically if she was prophetic, in several instances to the point that the couple ended up separating. They enjoy the role of matchmaker, trying to tell members who to marry or that your spouse is the wrong person for you.

They take pleasure in exercising control over the destiny of members, implying that God has to speak to them first about your destiny. They like to make you feel that they are the ones who need to release you into your destiny and that you need them in order to fulfil your destiny. They may even require that their members' personal decisions be approved by them first, and if they're not then they are ignored or ridiculed.

In terms of their personality traits, Jezebelic leaders have a tendency to be flirtatious, although this doesn't apply to them all. They love secrecy and are habitual liars with a deceptive spirit. They're hypercritical of others and love to project their own weaknesses onto others. They will often abuse favors and privileges that have been extended to them, acting in an entitled manner.

Financially speaking, these leaders require that members or those who seek their favor pay their personal bills, take them to lunch, and so on. I'm not referring to the tithes here, but to expenses beyond that. They will favor members who are flourishing financially.

Witchcraft-type leaders will lead via control. In these church environments, there is usually spiritual abuse. Oftentimes, people are under witchcraft-type leaders without realizing it because the manner of leadership has become normal. It is only when they move from such environments do they recognize the level of bondage they were under.

On the other hand, there may be members who recognize that they are under a witchcraft leader. They, however, stay and try to make things work or have managed to convince themselves that they can be a source of change. This can appear to be a simple task since such leaders are not bad through and through—they also possess finer traits. However, let's remember witchcraft is rooted in the belief system of an individual. It will take nothing less than the power of Holy Spirit to penetrate and unravel that system.

If you are a leader and you find that you have checked several traits of a witchcraft leader, please know that God brought this information to you because he wants to correct you. Proverbs 3:12 says, "For whom the Lord loves He corrects, Just as a father the son in whom he delights."

To walk in freedom in this area, you will need to reach out to your leader, a mentor, or someone with whom you have an accountability relationship who is also confidential, able to counsel you and take you through deliverance, or accompany you to those who can take you through deliverance. This individual should also be able to walk you through to victory.

The final phase is critical and should not be taken for granted. Establishing an accountability relationship is wise since it will help in preventing you from defaulting while simultaneously providing encouragement and support.

Anyone who has been under a witchcraft leader, especially for a prolonged period of time, will also need to go through deliverance. Being in a witchcraft environment causes psychological trauma. This is internal damage, and it should not be ignored. Collins English Dictionary (online) defines "trauma" as *a very severe shock or very upsetting experience, which may cause psychological damage.* Too many times, believers go through traumatic experiences, but they either ignore it or try to pray it away. Not everything can be prayed away. In some instances, deliverance and counseling may be necessary in order for you to enjoy the quality of life Christ desires that you have. Here are some mental residues of being under a witchcraft leader:

- Low self-esteem
- Feeling of rejection
- Feelings of inadequacy
- Spiritual and emotional abuse
- Suicidal
- Aborts destiny
- Delayed destiny
- Financial distress
- Depression
- Sickness
- Insomnia
- Fear

Here is some wisdom: it's a huge challenge to cause change to flow from the bottom up. Do not remain in a witchcraft environment with the belief that you can change it. This is self-deception. The only change that you can absolutely influence is that concerning your own life.

Prosperity Preachers and Witchcraft

Before I continue, I would like to make it clear that I believe in giving, sowing, and tithing. However, I've attended church services in which people were manipulated into giving and in most cases, by people who claimed to have an anointing for prosperity. Compelling people to give is not scriptural. I don't care what anointing you have. God did not anoint anyone to extract money from or manipulate his people into giving. Spiritual giving is done out of free will. Giving out of compulsion or having to give offering multiple times during the same service because the preacher feels you could have given a better offering. I am sorry, but did any of these preachers put a better offering in anyone's pocket? This is witchcraft!

This is my take on giving: "Each of you should give what you have decided in your heart to give, not reluctantly or under compulsion, for God loves a cheerful giver." (2 Corinthians 9:7) We cannot go wrong when we stick to the Word. I understand there are situations in which a leader may ask the people to give a bit more—let's say there is an event such as a conference, and all of the expenses have not been covered—in such situations, sure. And I understand that there are times that the leader of a church may challenge the people to give a special offering or sow a seed of a specific amount. I am not referring to such situations. I am talking about those who think that they are anointed to extract people's hard-earned cash from their pockets by twisting Scriptures and boasting of an anointing that has a questionable scent. Also, if you are a visiting preacher, don't go raising a special offering without proper permission from the leader of that church. And, leaders do not collaborate with visiting speakers to extract money from those you lead. It's wicked.

Shielding Prophets in Your Ministry from Witchcraft

Firstly, let me say this: Prophets are not more special than anyone else. However, in most cases, the warfare they face is different from everyone else. Jezebel hates prophets! I've explained the reason for this earlier, and I've also given clear signs of a witchcraft attack. Leaders, it's your role to cover all of those you lead, including your prophets. In order to lead effectively, and especially if you are going to raise up five-folders, it's critical that you have an understanding of each office and the challenges and warfare those who occupy them will face so that you can effectively give wisdom, guidance, and covering. Ignorance is one of your strongest enemies. When you don't understand the attacks a five-folder may face, it's highly possible that you join the warfare against that individual whom you should be fighting with.

Leaders do not be the enemy within the gates. Don't fight nor compete with your prophets. Prophets flow better with apostles. A prophet will most likely struggle in a pastor-alone church environment because prophets tend to be God-focused, while pastors tend to be people-focused. Therefore, these two offices will not always understand each other. With that being said, if you are an apostle, by virtue of the office, a prophet may prophesy more, with greater depth, authority or accuracy. They will see more, hear more, dream more. People may even be more attracted to them because of the gift. This is no reason to be alarmed. They will not have the grace to lead like you because God has set you as leader over the house. Don't be intimidated. Instead, give wisdom, guidance, rebuke and correction as needed, but always as a leader never as a competitor.

Secondly, your prophets will come under attacks of slander, accusations, and lies, some more than others. An attack is not a reflection of the prophet's character; it's a strategy of the enemy. Always be conscious of the difference. Also, you cannot give leadership in the good times and distance yourselves in the challenging times—you might as well not be a leader at all. Your role as a leader includes protecting or covering. Encyclopedia.com defines "covering" *as a thing used to cover something else; typically, in order to protect or conceal it.* Therefore, it's your role to cover your prophets through prayer and stand with them during times of attack. The spirit of witchcraft likes to operate in secret. Do not open the door to secrecy. It's a demonic portal. Those with a witchcraft spirit will come to you or a member of your ministry to share in secret concerning one of your prophets. Do not receive an accusation in the absence of the accused. The church is probably the only place where this is tolerated. Here is a simple approach:

- Call a meeting. Require that all parties be present and ask the accuser to walk with evidence to support their claims, if possible.

A friend once related to me how one member of her ministry brought an accusation against another member. The member bringing the accusation had quite a bit to say. This friend related that in an attempt to be fair to the individual being accused, she indicated to the member bringing the accusation that she will call a meeting and invite a few other individuals along with the member being accused. The member bringing the accusation said, "no!" She was adamant; she did not want the accused there. She threatened that if the accused is invited to the meeting, she will not attend! My friend let her know that if the accused cannot be present, then everything communicated about the individual will be treated as invalid. However, not everyone will shrink back in such situations. Some will be bold-faced liars.

Dealing with accusations in an open, transparent manner shuts the door to scandal and gossip. Leaders are key gatekeepers in such situations. Whether it's on the job or in the justice system, when someone is accused, they are required to be present. The church should not be that place where people are tried and sentenced in their absence. Accusation received in the absence of the accused is called "gossip," and responsible leaders should not tolerate gossip. Call a meeting with all concerned. Don't worry; you will not be overwhelmed with meetings. Rather, people will think many times before they approach you with an accusation. Here is my recommended approach:

- Take and keep the lead in the meeting. Someone with a witchcraft personality will try to dominate the meeting and steer it in the direction that they want it to go. They may also keep you bouncing around from one issue to the next, without allowing you to resolve anything. It's their strategy of taking control and staying undetected.
- Expect emotional outbursts, whether its anger or tears. In most cases, it's an attempt to manipulate you or others in the meeting. Don't be moved by it.
- Ask all present to turn off all of their electronic devices or leave them out of the meeting area. I've known of individuals secretly recording such meetings, then editing them to suit their needs. If you, as the leader want to make a recording of the meeting, make it known to all involved.
- Listen to the Holy Spirit during such meetings. This is very critical. The Holy Spirit will unveil hidden things to you during such times, guide you on how to approach such situations, and even tell you what to say at times.
- Correct if necessary, but don't demean your prophets, especially in the presence of others. Also, don't demean someone you are assigned to cover to satisfy someone who is not under your leadership. I've witnessed situations in which accusations were laid against prophets and their leaders, without ever having discussions or verifying information, began demeaning their prophets based on the information received. The end result was that the prophets lost confidence in their leader's ability to cover them and those who brought the accusations vowed never to attend the ministry because of the treatment they'd witnessed being meted out to a member based on something that was false.

Traits of a Jezebelic Member

Jezebelic members often show up as an answer to prayer, with the right skill set and gifts your church is lacking. For this reason, it's wise not to give people positions and assignments too early. Allow them to sit for a while and prove their commitment to the vision of the church without a position.

They like to get involved in the early stages of a ministry or a team within the ministry. Thus, they will eagerly volunteer.

They like to think they are right and everyone else is wrong or is against them.

If they are a part of a ministry team in the church, they tend to be critical of leadership. Thus, they may frequently take complaints to higher leadership or set themselves up as the unofficial leader of the team.

Expect rebellion. Bear in mind that rebellion is not always bold opposition. Sometimes, it shows up as another way of doing a task instead of following what the leader requested. It may be a good idea, but it was not what was requested.

They will encourage you to question, challenge, or rebel against God-ordained leadership.

They are assassins of prophets or prophetic leaders. Jezebel has a mandate to kill true prophets and, by extension, the true prophetic. They will accuse, scandal, seduce, and use every possible weapon in their witchcraft arsenal to get the head of leadership. John the Baptist lost his head because of Jezebelic Herodias. Matthew 14:6-10 records the following: "But when Herod's birthday was celebrated, the daughter of Herodias danced before them and pleased Herod. Therefore, he promised with an oath to give her whatever she might ask. So she, having been prompted by her mother, said, 'Give me

John the Baptist's head here on a platter.' And the king was sorry; nevertheless, because of the oaths and because of those who sat with him, he commanded *it* to be given to *her.* So he sent and had John beheaded in prison." (NKJV) Herodias hated John the Baptist because he confronted Herod about his relationship with her. Prophets cannot help but confront sin. Those with Jezebelic personalities hate confrontation, as they prefer to be quiet and try to function under the leader's radar. The moment they are confronted, they will manifest and become openly murderous. This is what happened with Herodias. She was looking for an opportunity to take the head of God's prophet. Then the opportunity came, and she seized it. Prophets and prophetic leaders, Jezebel will settle for nothing less than your head! This spirit is ruthless and does not negotiate or make peace treaties. Do not attempt to counsel and coexist with a Jezebel.

With that being said, leaders should always be conscious of the fact that Jezebel cannot function without an Ahab and vice versa. Thus, these two personalities will magnetize. Leaders should never allow Jezebel and Ahab to form an alliance. This could be disastrous!

Confrontation is the only way to resolve witchcraft and Jezebelic situations in the church. If not, everything will be undermined and contaminated. Harboring members with Jezebelic personalities, especially if they are in full manifestation mode, alters the atmosphere in the church. The atmosphere becomes heavy and you can literally feel the stress and manipulation. Leadership will need to confront such situations quickly. Confrontation is not for the faint of heart—it gets messy. It will require the leader being firm and uncompromising in their decision. There will be those who will conclude that the leader is too harsh. Such confrontations are never about emotion and sentiments, but they are about saving the vision and integrity of the church. If the leader loses their head, everything will suffer or die. Here is how I suggest confrontation be approached:

Call a meeting. Invite three sets of people—the parties concerned, in other words, everyone connected with whatever is currently happening. You also need to invite witnesses, who could be one or a few neutral people. You should also invite the secretary of the church board. This person's role is to formally record the meeting.

During the actual meeting, the leader should take and keep the lead of the meeting. The leader should also raise whatever issue they are currently dealing with in clear, precise language. Witchcraft personalities like to speak in a hazy, confusing manner. The leader should not allow it. Keep all communication clear and not be moved by emotional outbursts. One of the greatest challenges with individuals who function out of witchcraft is that they think they are right, therefore, repentance or acknowledging their wrongdoing does not happen easily. If a member is unrepentant in their attack against leadership, then the leaders have and should exercise every right to ask such a member to leave the church.

After such individual leaves, the leader will need to take the church through a time of healing and restoration through several processes.

Intercessory prayer will be needed so that emotional healing flows. Leaders bleed, and I know that many leaders think that acknowledging that they were hurt or suffered trauma by such an attack is a sign of weakness. This is not true. Rather, it shows that you have a soul. You don't have to be weak and weeping in front of the people you lead but, alone with the Lord, you can be as broken as you need to be.

Another thing that adds to the grief of a leader during such times is the judgment they face by those who were not directly involved, such as peers and associates. Such individuals often conclude that the leader was too harsh and acted without love. Thus, sometimes, it becomes a painful, lonely journey to recovery.

Intercessory prayer has to be made not only for the leader but also for the remaining members who were directly involved as they too were hurt and traumatized. Then there is a group who gets overlooked—those church members who were not involved, but they may have heard the rumors and felt the strife. They too were hurt by the impact of the attack; thus, they should not be neglected during times of prayer.

Spiritual warfare is critical because it pulls down demonic and anointing-opposing altars that were erected during the time of witchcraft manifestation. This activity also drives out any lingering spirit of witchcraft and rebellion and uproots demonic seeds planted in the minds of people.

Prophetic worship restores the atmosphere by refocusing members on the person of Jesus; on His holiness, majesty, and beauty and rekindles a love and passion for Christ.

Vision casting helps members to gather themselves and refocus on the mission and assignment of the church. It also reconnects them to their individual roles.

Reflection for Church Leaders

1. What steps should I take to ensure I do not function out of witchcraft?
2. What steps should I take to ensure the prophets and prophetic people under my leadership function in a Jezebel-free zone?
3. What strategy do I have to use to slam shut every demonic portal of secrecy in the church?

Prayer and Declaration for Leaders

Father, in the name of Jesus, I pray that those You place in my care will thrive. Help me to never lead by control but by the leading of the Holy Spirit and Your inspired Word; be it prophetic or written. Grant me eyes to see, the heart to discern, and the ear to hear the enemy from afar. Anoint my hands to defeat Jezebel when this spirit roars against those you have assigned me to lead. Amen.

Chapter 6:

Witchcraft in the Family

Often, draped in the façade of era and culture, the spirit of witchcraft has targeted the family to attempt to unravel its God-ordained structure. Thus, attempts are being made to blot out the roles for husband, wife, and children as set down by God. However, God's standards for family structure transcend the current trends of our times, and they stand as the authority over and the prescription for all of our modern madness.

Role of the Husband and Wife in Marriage

1 Corinthians 11:3 says, "But I want you to realize that the head of every man is Christ, and the head of the woman is man, and the head of Christ is God." (NIV) I do not believe that God created women lesser in value or purpose than men. Genesis 5:2 tells us, "Male and female created he them; and blessed them, and called their name Adam, in the day when they were created." (KJV) The name "Adam" which means *humankind*, was an identification given by God to the two people He created. These people came from the earth that they were assigned to govern and have authority over. The name "Adam' made both the male and female equal in value and relevance.

However, they were different in function. Genesis 2:18 says, "And the Lord God said, "*It is* not good that man should be alone; I will make him a helper comparable to him." (NKJV) Although the wife is comparable or as good as her husband in the value she brings to the marriage, her God-assigned role is to be a helper to her husband. He was set in authority over her.

The woman being assigned as helper tells me that the man already had an assigned role. With that being said, it is critical that we understand that "helper" is not the *identification* of the woman; it's simply her *function*. "Helper" is not *who* she is; it's what she *does*. Outside the marital structure, the woman can fulfill any role.

Fast forward to today. The challenge many wives face is that their husbands want to rightfully occupy their seat of authority in marriage and family life, but they seriously lack when it comes to fulfilling their responsibility of being head of the woman and by extension, of the home. The woman's role of helper to her husband comes from a posture of being in submission to him. Genuine submission is always powered by respect; and if a husband cannot fulfill his role as leader, then his wife will have challenges submitting to him.

Because of the aforementioned, some women morph into witchcraft personalities over a period of time to compensate for the lack of leadership in the home. I am not saying that all women who find themselves in such situations have witchcraft personalities. I am saying that some adapt their personality to cope with the situation they face. On the other hand, many women have very responsible husbands. Such women simply enter marriage with witchcraft personalities or develop same during the marriage.

A wife may be controlling at home but willingly submits to the authority of her male boss, spiritual leader, or some other male authority figure because of these men's consistent show of strength and prowess. However, here lies the deception. In marriage, a woman may be more conscious of and even overwhelmed by those areas of deficiency in her husband. Outside of marriage, she is presented with the imagery of masculine strength and competence. Seduced by the contrast, she undervalues, dishonors, and dominated her husband without pausing long enough to realize that the same irresponsible behavior her husband displays may very well be displayed by the men she admires in their own marriages.

Every challenge has a solution, and this type of challenge is no different. In situations like this, the wife and helper can "help" her husband by humbly and gently pointing him to his role. She can also study pertinent Scriptures with him and pray with and for him. She could even try to convince him to attend couples' counseling, depending on the gravity of the situation.

Controlling Traits That Can Manifest in Either Spouse

- Public humiliation
- Not allowing spouse to fulfill their God-ordained destiny
- Guilt trips
- Initiating quarrels
- Hostility
- Influencing children against each other
- Abusive language
- Threatening divorce
- Speaking in a condescending manner

Traits of a Controlling Husband

- Physical abuse
- Other traits of a male Jezebel that are listed in Chapter 2

Traits of a Controlling Wife

- Rationing or completely withholding sex
- Demanding to manage her husband's finances
- Pouting or crying if she cannot have her way
- Threatening to involve her family members in minute marital disagreements
- Not submissive: A wife submits by yielding her soul and body to her husband. Thus, the lack of submission can be reflected in but not limited to her attitude, tone, and body language.
- Pretending to be sick
- Not allowing her husband to have friends
- Not allowing her husband to have communication with his relatives

Traits of Controlling Children

Young children can push the boundaries to see how far they can go; thus, any sign of controlling traits needs to be nipped in the bud by means of instruction and discipline. Here are a few signs that your children are attempting to tip the scales of control in their favor:

- Tantrums (This goes especially for toddlers and pre-toddlers.)
- Pouting
- Ignoring parents
- Isolating themselves
- Threatening to run away
- Threatening to commit suicide
- Threatening to become pregnant
- Using drugs
- Staying out late
- Refusing to follow instructions

In-Laws

The family also comes under the attack of witchcraft from in-laws. This area is like the elephant in the room for many marriages, but no one wants to touch that elephant for fear of the shaking that could occur. However, let's poke that elephant for a bit, shall we?

Let's see what God says concerning the children and parents' relationship. "Children, obey your parents in the Lord, for this is right. 'Honor your father and mother,' which is the first commandment with promise: 'that it may be well with you and you may live long on the earth.'" (Ephesians 6:1-3 NKJV) Now, let's have some clarity regarding this portion of Scripture.

"Children obey your parents" refers to young children—not adult children and not married children. Thus, parents have no right to impose their will or desires on their adult children. Parents can make suggestions, and they can share their opinions or ideas to the extent that it was requested and to the extent that it is permitted. Anything beyond that is crossing boundaries.

Adult children should not be pressured or made to feel guilty to the point that they give in to their parents' wishes. Some parents like to make their children feel guilty and obligated to surrender their free will by reminding them of all of the things they have done for them and all of the sacrifices they have made. However, if you brought someone into this world, it's your responsibility to take care of them to the best of your ability until they are able to do so for themselves. Parents taking care of their children is not a favor. It's a responsibility. Children shouldn't be giving their parents rewards for being responsible.

"Honor your father and mother." Children of all ages should honor their parents. This means that parents should be held in high esteem and treated with respect in spite of their imperfections. They should partake of any blessings and privileges their children experience. As far as possible, adult children should take care of elderly parents.

In-Laws and Boundaries

There are more people with challenges when it comes to relationship with in-laws, than not. There are clear guidelines in the Word regarding marriage, and if we follow those guidelines, the challenges will be reduced. Let's apply the principles regarding the law of first mentions as it relates to marriage.

"And the Lord God caused a deep sleep to fall on Adam, and he slept; and He took one of his ribs and closed up the flesh in its place. Then the rib which the Lord God had taken from man He made into a woman, and He brought her to the man. And Adam said: "This *is* now bone of my bones and flesh of my flesh; she shall be called Woman, Because she was taken out of Man." Therefore a man shall leave his father and mother and be joined to his wife, and they shall become one flesh." (Genesis 2:21-24 NKJV)

God brought Eve to Adam, and thus, we have the first marriage. At this marriage, Adam made a proclamation, thereby giving the governing principles regarding marriage. For the reason of marriage shall a man leave his parents and be joined to his wife. Leaving and being joined are critical transition points.

Leave physically: It's not advisable that couples marry and live with their parents as this opens the door to undesired interference and opportunities for control.

It's not always the mother who becomes the Jezebel in-law, sometimes it's an older sister. I know of a family situation in which one of the older (but not the eldest) sisters is the witchcraft personality. She controls all of her siblings; both males and females. She decides where they go to church, what activities they get involved in that church, who their friends are, and who they marry. She also manages the lives of her nieces and nephews. Her sisters live with her, and although her brothers live separately, they or their wives must visit her house at least once a day. Because of her control, all of her female siblings have grown old and remain unmarried. Her male siblings have difficult marriages. They are physically abusive to their wives, and she finds reasons to validate it. Some are unfaithful to their wives, and she befriends the other women. Some of her brothers are now divorced. When an individual is this controlling, it good to live far away and keep communication to the minimum.

Leave emotionally: Sometimes, a spouse can be so attached to a parent that it becomes unhealthy for their marriage. Cut the umbilical cord—grow up. Love your mama but let go of her apron. Women find this trait distasteful in men.

Leave financially: It's not wise to marry if you are not financially stable. If your parents support you financially, then they have the right to ask difficult questions and give firm instructions.

"Be joined" means:

- Unchallenged commitment to your spouse. Love your parents and siblings, but your commitment is with your spouse.
- The couple develops their own culture. The parents or siblings of neither of the couple get to dictate how things are done in the marriage, how the couple raise their children, how monies are spent, how the home is decorated, and so on.
- Freedom to love and lavish. In-laws, especially women, consider it perfectly loving when they are loved and lavished by their spouse; but if their son or brother loves and lavishes his wife, they are very critical and even suspicious.

Signs of Witchcraft from In-Laws

- Invent ways to cause their child to remain dependent on them.
- Consistently giving errands and asking favors of their adult child.
- Requiring that their child seek approval for their choice of marriage partner.
- Requiring that their child seeks their approval for personal decisions.
- Creating a feeling of guilt and obligation.
- Often criticizing their child's spouse.
- Using supernatural forms of witchcraft against the spouse of their child.
- Assassinating the character of their child's spouse. This is done by creating a false image of and communicating false information about this individual.
- Playing the victim.
- Speaking to their child's spouse in a demeaning or sarcastic manner.
- Attempting to influence a grandchild or the grandchildren against one or both of their parents.
- Shutting out their child's spouse from family gatherings and conversations.

- Completely ignoring their child's spouse.
- Never talking directly to their child's spouse.
- Making accusations against their child's spouse.
- Acting as though they are entitled to receive preferential treatment over spouse, children of their child, or sibling.

Every form of control can be cut off by setting clear boundaries. Boundaries are rules and expectations you set for your parents, siblings, and even relatives to follow regarding how they relate to and interact with your spouse and children.

Reflection

1. Am I a controlling spouse?
2. Or am I a supportive spouse?
3. Are there clearly established boundaries around my marriage and family?
4. Do I consistently honor the boundaries set around my marriage and family?

Prayer and Declaration

Father, I pray that peace and prosperity will be within the wall of my marriage and that my family will function according to Your design throughout all generations and in spite of any contrary trend of the present era.

I declare that my children are strong and established in the ways of the Lord and that our legacy of righteousness is preserved, in Jesus' name. Amen.

Chapter 7:

Getting to the Roots

The origin of the spirit of Jezebel in an individual's life is like the root of a tree. It grows and flourishes because it's nourished and anchored by a source. Let's also remember that this spirit establishes itself in the mental structure of an individual. Therefore, to experience deliverance, this structure has to be uprooted and a new structure erected. As mentioned earlier, a mental structure or stronghold is erected when specific thought patterns are accepted and networked into the identity of an individual, thus influencing their belief system, behaviors, and lifestyle. It is critical that we look into that structure in order to recognize how the spirit has taken control.

Roots of a Controlling Behavior

Before I continue, I want to encourage you. If you recognize that you have controlling traits, do not allow the enemy to cause you to feel condemned. Two of my goals for writing this book are to equip and edify the saints so that they walk in freedom. Thus, this book was written for your benefit. Also, do not allow pride to rise up in your heart, causing you to overlook your controlling behavior.

Rejection: This is one of the primary ways that this spirit networks itself into an individual's mind. Rejection can start as early as the womb and be repeatedly reinforced over the years into adulthood. It can come from any source; from parent to pastor and other individuals in between. We were designed with the need to feel loved and accepted; and when this basic need is not met, mindsets and behaviors are consciously and subconsciously developed as coping mechanisms. Unfortunately, demonic spirits, not only Jezebel, use these mechanisms as doorways into the lives of the rejected.

While on earth, Jesus Christ experienced rejection on many occasions and on many levels so that you may know; by experience, the acceptance, and the love of your Heavenly Father. John 1:12: "But as many as received him, to them gave the power to become the sons of God, even to them that believe on his name." (KJV) It is by embracing the fact that we are sons of God that the doorway to rejection is closed.

One of the things that no one prepares us for during prophetic mentorship is rejection. Prophets will face rejection. This is why prophets always need to understand and remember the distinction between their identity and their function. Prophets are sons of God who are called to function in the office of the prophet. *Prophet* is not who we are; we are sons of God. *Prophet* is a function. Therefore, when we are functioning in our office and someone rejects a message we deliver, we should not feel rejected. Why should the delivery guy feel rejected because the recipient of a package refuses to accept that package? The guy doesn't care. He just moves on.

Prophets feel rejected when their prophetic utterances are not accepted because they have wrapped their identity in their function. This is why we have people running around with their chests in the air, saying, "I am a prophet" but the moment someone says, "no" to their utterance, they are deflated and sitting in a corner.

Sometimes, even before we know who we are, the enemy already knows; thus, he sets cycles of demonic patterns to derail us from destiny. Based on my observation, rejection is one of those demonic patterns in the lives of many prophets, and it starts from childhood. I believe that deliverance is a continuous process, and it should be a part of prophetic mentoring. Prophets in training need to be able to discern areas of woundedness and demonic doorways in their lives and be delivered from them. If a prophet already had roots of rejection, the root is only reinforced when he experiences rejection functioning in his office. In such situations, it becomes easy for that prophet to morph into a Jezebelic personality.

Extreme Insecurity: This can be a manifestation of or a doorway to rejection. This doorway can be closed in the same way that the doorway to rejection is closed.

Bitterness: If not quickly uprooted, bitterness will grow into a demonic tree and a seat for Jezebel to be enthroned upon. Bitterness springs from offense; whether real or perceived. Opportunities to be offended will always present themselves. We can choose to accept offense or reject it. However, if bitterness has already found its way into your heart, there is only one thing left to do—get rid of it! "Let all bitterness, wrath, anger, clamor, and evil speaking be put away from you, with all malice." (Ephesians 4:31 KJV)

Resentment: This can be caused by the feelings of jealously towards someone because of their success, constantly being overlooked by those in authority, unresolved conflicts, offense, disappointment, or hurt. Resentment is the twin of bitterness.

Hurts: These are deep emotional wounds that can be caused by betrayal, disappointment, abandonment, rejection, physical or emotional abuse, and so on.

Childhood wounds: These can be caused by physical abuse, sexual abuse, abandonment, disapproval and criticism, having a domineering parent or caregiver, broken promises, witnessing a parent being abused, divorce of parents, among others.

Poor parental relationships: On every occasion where I have encountered a Jezebelic or an Ahab personality, that individual always had a rocky relationship with at least one of their parents. I have observed that Jezebelic personalities were rejected by, felt rejected by, or had a struggling relationship with their father. On the other hand, an Ahab personality was rejected by, felt rejected by, or had a struggling relationship with their mother. Hence, Ahab personalities tend to gravitate towards Jezebelic female personalities or women with strong personalities. The aforementioned may not be applicable in every instance; however, it's a pattern I have observed.

Idolatry: Idolatry in any form, will open an individual's life to demonic influence and control. As it relates to the spirit of Jezebel, demonic doorways can be opened by worshipping Mary (The mother of Jesus Christ). Baal worship is another doorway. This is the worship of self-will. Thus, such individuals will exalt their will over others. Another doorway is self-worship; this is the "Queen Bee" syndrome. The spoilt child of the parents or family can come under the influence of the spirit of Jezebel. Also, a priestess; a devotee or anyone who is dedicated to the service of a deity is wide open for the spirit of Jezebel to be enthroned in their life.

Inheritance: The last root of controlling behavior we'll examine is inheritance. An individual could inherit the spirit of witchcraft if their behavior was molded and influenced by a Jezebelic parent or grandparent. This spirit can also be inherited from any form of leadership or influential personality, whether it's in the church or otherwise.

Also, a child can inherit a spirit of witchcraft from a parent who was or is involved in the occult. When the child gets saved, the spirit simply changes its form from being occultic in nature to being a controlling spirit.

Deliverance

After examining the roots of controlling behavior, an individual may recognize that they have more than one root or that a specific root was being reinforced in their lives. It is important to understand that one or more demonic roots only serve to strengthen the demonic network. Ultimately, our deliverance is our responsibility. To be free of demonic roots, we need to:

- Embrace deliverance as an opportunity to be free. Pride will keep you in bondage.
- Examine your life. Reflect on your personal history and your family history for demonic roots and uproot them.
- Seek deliverance to drive out demons from your life.

Destroy Negative Mental Strongholds

It's important to destroy negative mental strongholds as soon as they've been identified. This is done by recognizing and rejecting negative thought patterns, replacing them with positive affirmations from the Word of God. It's important to repent and completely change the way you think by consistently meditating on the Word of God, accepting its truth into your heart. This will help you change the way you speak, "for the mouth speaks what the heart is full of" (Luke 6:45 NIV UK). This will be followed by a change in lifestyle as you allow the Word of God and the counsel of the Holy Spirit to guide you in your daily activities. Make sure you resist the temptation to default to old behaviors but remain consistent as you establish new habits in your life. It's vitally important through this process to remember to honor the right of others to exercise free will, and for you to submit to those who have God-ordained authority over you.

Reflection

1. Have I identified any root of controlling behavior in my life?
2. Are there roots of rejection in my life?
3. Am I willing to make seeking deliverance a priority?

Prayer and Declaration

Father, I thank you for healing and deliverance in every area in my mind that the enemy has established a stronghold, in Jesus' name. Amen.

Chapter 8:

The Spirit of Jezebel and Feminism

King of Moab

Balak, king of the Moabites, hired Balaam, a prophet, to curse the people of God. The people had settled next to his territory on their way to Canaan. Balak was afraid and distressed by the number and might of God's people.

However, Balaam could not curse God's people because Yahweh had already blessed them. Yahweh counseled Balaam against cursing his people. Further, it's obvious that Balaam would not release a word God did not give him. "But Balaam answered and said to the servants of Balak, "Though Balak were to give me his house full of silver and gold, I could not go beyond the command of the Lord my God to do less or more." Numbers 22:18

But Balak did not give up; instead, he became ever more persistent. He kept sending to Balaam princes who were more honorable than the previous emissary. We must observe that the enemy does not easily give up and walks away, defeated. I used the word "emissary" deliberately. The online Oxford Living Dictionaries defines "emissary" as a *person sent as a diplomatic representative on a special mission.*

The Greek word *apostolos* was a naval term that described an admiral, the fleet of ships that travelled with him, along with the accompanying specialized crew. The fleet was "sent" to find "uncivilized" territories. Once such a territory was located, the admiral; referred to as the *apostolos* accompanied by his crew began their mission of colonizing that "uncivilized" territory into a replica of the country they represent. Hence, emissary, ambassador, diplomat, and representative are relative words as it relates to being "sent" on a specialized mission by God, a king, or the government. Balak sent his princes on a specialized mission; to persuade Balaam the prophet to accompany them, to curse God's people. God sent his Son Jesus Christ to earth on a specialized mission; to redeem mankind back to Himself. It's important that the Church understands that the spirit of Jezebel is apostolic in nature. "Apostolic" is a derivate of the word "apostle." This spirit was "sent" to infiltrate and overthrow godly systems, structures, and leadership then colonize and govern the assigned territory.

When an apostle is sent to a territory, that "sent one" is mandated by God to dislodge any ruling principality and establish that territory as kingdom territory, with all of the necessary visible manifestations of change in rulership. While the Church has acknowledged that the spirit of Jezebel hates prophets and prophetic people in general, we should not ignore the reality that this spirit is apostolic in nature and assignment. Balak not only persisted in sending emissaries but sent a higher rank every time he received a negative report.

It was believed that prophets like Balaam were hired because they knew how to negotiate with national gods, even turning them against their own people by means of rituals, offerings, and sacrifices.

When Balaam finally accompanied Balak to curse the people of God, only blessing came out of his mouth. Balak, however, did not relent. He kept building altars, offering even more extravagant sacrifices and convincing Balaam to make another attempt to curse the people of Yahweh.

The Spirit of Jezebel and Feminism

From Balak's confession, it appears as though Balaam had a reputation as it relates to blessing and cursing. "Come now, curse this people for me, since they are too mighty for me. Perhaps I shall be able to defeat them and drive them from the land, for I know that he whom you bless is blessed, and he whom you curse is cursed." Numbers 22:6. Balak placed his confidence in the reputation that this pagan prophet carried. Thus, he consistently pursued him. But Balaam could not curse God's people. However, he counselled Balak how to cause Israel to sin, which would result in Yahweh cursing them. The counsel was effective.

Israel's Apostasy

Moses was angry with the officers of the army—the commanders of thousands and commanders of hundreds—who returned from the battle. "Have you allowed all the women to live?" he asked them. "They were the ones who followed Balaam's advice and enticed the Israelites to be unfaithful to the Lord in the Peor incident, so that a plague struck the Lord's people." Numbers 31:14-16.

Balaam's advice, it seemed, was to send the women of Moab to entice the men of Israel. Once the men became enticed, the people of God would have been infiltrated, compromised, and ultimately cursed by Yahweh. "While Israel lived in Shittim, the people began to whore with the daughters of Moab. These invited the people to the sacrifices of their gods, and the people ate and bowed down to their gods. So, Israel yoked himself to Baal of Peor. And the anger of the Lord was kindled against Israel." Numbers 25:1-3. The online Bible Dictionary describes Baal Peor as: *lord of the openings, a god of the Moabites, worshipped by obscene rites*. So called from Mount Peor, where this worship was celebrated, the Baal of Peor. The Israelites fell into the worship of this idol.

The worship of Baal Peor was built around sexual acts. The worship of Baal Peor was also matriarchal in nature, meaning women played the dominant role in temple worship since there was not a great divide between worship and social culture, as in the 21st century. This meant the society was very matriarchal, opposed to Israel, which was very patriarchal. Observe that Numbers 25:3 said, "... Israel yoked *himself* to Baal of Peor. (emphasis added)

Baal Peor or Baal of Peor was another variation of the pagan deity, Baal. Peor was a mountain in Moab. In antiquity, it was believed that the gods dwelt in the mountains, away from where people lived or in luxuriant gardens. In Moab, Baal was worshipped on the mountain of Peor, as mentioned in an earlier chapter. Baal means *lord, husband, owner, master.* Women who functioned as Baal temple prostitutes are given to Baal as objects of worship. Hence, Baal is their lord, master, husband, and owner. They are not only submitted to but are in union with Baal. No doubt that these women were very sensual and seductive in conduct and attire.

A married woman given to a deity is usually not submissive to her husband as she ought to be. Rather, she assumes a domineering role. As mentioned in an earlier chapter, the name Jezebel means *unhusbanded, uninhabited.* Jezebel, the woman, could not have been joined to Ahab in the way that a woman should be jointed to her husband—in submission. This is because Jezebel was already jointed to Baal.

Jezebel Was "Sent"

As I mentioned earlier in this chapter, the spirit of Jezebel is apostolic in nature. Jezebel, the woman, the daughter of the high priest of Baal, king of the Sidonians, and keeper of the secrets of Baal sent his daughter Jezebel to Israel as an ambassador of Baal. She was sent to rule. Anytime someone is sent to rule or govern, that person needs to rebel against and overthrow the existing government.

In the Old Testament period, the nation of Israel was governed by the king, priest, and prophet. The king ruled on behalf of Yahweh, the priest maintained the temple and made offerings and sacrifices to Yahweh, and the prophet spoke on behalf of Yahweh. And even though the office of the Apostle was not there, the mandate existed. Jezebel, the woman, married the king of Israel and killed Yahweh's prophets. She had a demonic apostolic anointing. In addition to driving terror in the hearts of the prophets of Yahweh and mercilessly slaughtered them, Jezebel sent Elijah; a mighty prophet of the Most High God, under a juniper tree, begging God to take his life.

In the New Testament, the Church government is the five-fold: apostle, prophet, evangelist, pastor, and teacher. According to Ephesians 2:20, the Church is "built on the foundation of the apostles and prophets, Christ Jesus himself being the cornerstone." A building is condemned or destroyed once the foundation has been compromised or weakened. The spirit of Jezebel targets both components of the foundation—but differently. This spirit seeks to take the place of or replace true prophets and wage war with the apostles for the government of a territory.

And yes, we know marriages between royalties forged strong relationships. At first glance, it may appear as though this was the only thing happening when the Sidonian king married his daughter to the king of Israel. But there was a secret agenda. Jezebel's marriage to Ahab also had a spiritual dimension to it. Baal was actually infiltrating a nation Yahweh selected for himself. Jezebel's mission was to infiltrate the nation God selected for himself, rule that nation instead of its king, overthrow its established form of worship, and establish the worship of Baal.

Today, the mission remains the same. The spirit of Jezebel is sent by the god of this world to infiltrate the ecclesia—a people the Lord has called out to Himself—to seduce and deceive them to the point that they worship Baal in their church buildings, overthrow godly systems, structures, and leadership on every level; individual, corporate, and national to occupy the seat of government.

This spirit is mandated by Satan to govern. Since the Garden of Eden, it is quite clear that Satan is after man's God-given position of having dominion on earth. Since the fall in Eden, it's only those in covenant with the Most High God have been fully restored to that position of fully walking in their governmental authority on earth, under the Old Covenant—Israel; under the new covenant—the Church. The enemy knows where true authority is. The Lord taught me this: He said, "authority is never taken, it's given." In Eden, Adam and Eve gave their authority in exchange for knowledge of good and evil. At Peor, the men of Israel traded their status of being a blessed nation to that of falling under a plague because they allowed themselves to be seduced by sensual women. The church will do well to understand this—conquest is not always achieved by blood and battle. The enemy could wittingly send unsuspecting warriors. Everyone is a weapon or a potential weapon in the hand of the one who holds them.

The Feminine Weapon of War

The worship of Baal is the worship of self-will. The worship of Baal Peor was the worship of feminine sensuality, sexuality, and immoral lifestyle. This spirit of Baal Peor is already a part of social culture but is currently seeking to infiltrate and establish itself in the Church. Today, whether overt or covert, all sorts of sexual immorality and looseness is happening in the church, from pulpit to pew. Baal Peor has found or created a breach, and that breach needs to be closed. The church needs to rise up, dust itself off, and govern. While we must admit that not all have allowed themselves to be lured away to sin, too many have been bewitched.

The women of Moab were "sent" by their king on an apostolic mission; to entice the men of Israel and lure them away from being faithful to Yahweh into sexual immorality and other forms of pagan worship. Sexual immorality, in any form, is demonic in nature because sexual immorality is one of the various rituals or aspects of

Satan worship. From antiquity, the devils have been using sex and sensuality to lure and undermine godly structures such as marriage and family. The women of Moab were successful in their mission against the men of Israel by seducing them into pagan worship, which in turn resulted in Yahweh cursing the nation by sending a plague. In my opinion, that was radical feminism in all of its undignified glory. Let's see what it looks like in our time.

I will deflect a bit to say this: this disclosure is not for anyone to become paranoid or suspicious of every female who does not fit their impression of what a female should look or dress like. In today's culture, it's almost normal for unredeemed women to dress less modestly than in times past because of the shift in social norms. Also, oftentimes, women can innocently become victimized and weaponized by Satan when he sends spirits of seduction and lust to attach itself to them. Further, a woman can be appropriately dressed yet be the "sent" one. The enemy knows how to appropriately package his ambassadors. The purpose of this chapter is for the Church to recognize a spirit and another subtle but strong strategy of the enemy.

The Progression of Modern Feminism

Cambridge Online Dictionary defines feminism as "the belief that women should be allowed the same rights, power, and opportunities as men and be treated in the same way, or set of activities intended to achieve this state." In other words, feminism started well but has progressed. There were three waves of feminism before our current situation.

The First Wave of Feminism started in the 1800s, but accelerated late in the 1900s. During that era, married women had no legal identity or rights not even over their bodies. And basic privileges such as voting and owning properties were not available to them. This resulted in protests for the aforementioned. Consequently, most countries granted women the right to vote in the late 1800s. Other highlights of this era are: The Declaration of Sentiments being written, and the Planned Parenthood started under the name "Birth Control League."

The Second Wave of Feminism began in the 1960s. During this wave, many social norms were challenged, such as; the domination of patriarchy and gender inequality, workplace discrimination, segregated employment, and abortion laws. The inequality of pay between the genders was also challenged. Women fought for equal pay for equal work. This resulted in the Equal Pay Act being signed. During this wave, women gained a lot of success in their pursuits yet full equality eluded their grasp.

The Third Wave of Feminism came crashing in the 1990s, and girl power rode on its roar. This new breed of women found power and self-expression in their sexuality. This wave spread wider by including cultures and voices that were not represented in the first two waves. Therefore, it comes as no surprise that during this wave, strong, influential female icons in cartoons, movies, and in real life arose.

The Fourth Wave of Feminism sent a lot of barriers crashing down. Therefore, regardless of race, gender, class, and ethnicity, all are included. Feminists of this era hold the view that gender is a social construct. Self-love is promoted, and social restrictions and mindsets of the past relating to sexuality have been washed away. Many feminists in this wave hold the view that feminism is not misandry. Men have even encouraged join women in their pursuit to achieve economic, social, and political equality for all. Many are of the view that we are in the fourth wave.

The Weaponizing of Feminism

I believe feminism started with good intentions; women were fighting for their rights and equality. Today, we are crowned with their victories. However, I observed a subtle thing happening during the various waves. In a subtle way, undercurrent, the movement was and still being weaponized by Satan. I believe this is happening because the spirit of Jezebel has infiltrated this movement. The spirit of Jezebel promotes matriarchal dominance. A Peor—a mountain is being built for yet another variation of Baal to be worshipped.

I do not claim to be feminist in any way. But I do hold the view that God created male and female equally. I do not support women being suppressed, oppressed, or dominated because of their gender. I also believed that a married woman should be submitted to her husband, regardless of how successful or influential she is. Outside the marriage, she is free to pursue her goals and dreams, and shatter every glass ceiling she desires.

However, as women, in our pursuit for equality and freedom, we must be careful that we do not think that we are the new "male." And in gaining access to places previously dominated by men, we must be careful that we do not push men through the door and take complete control. Let's remember, "male and female created He them." We were created to coexist and work together. In this fourth wave, women must be careful that we do not resist being dominated so much, that we dominate our male counterparts.

Women have their own unique role to play in society and in God's plan for mankind. Therefore, it's pointless for women to invest time and energy trying to prove that they can do what a man can do. I am by no means saying that some women may not have genuine desires or should not infiltrate areas in society previously dominated by men. Nor am I saying that God cannot call women to function in leadership roles in the Body of Christ and function alongside of men.

Throughout the Bible, we see strong women like Deborah, who was a judge of Israel, a warrior, and a wife. Esther, the Jewish queen who saved her people from annihilation. Junia was the female apostle whom the apostle Paul considered noteworthy in Romans 16:7. Just to name a few.

I am saying, woman, be bold, be fierce, be feminine, but our assignment as women is not to replace men but function alongside of them. It's not about outdoing or winning—it's about drawing on each other's strength. Going out of the way to prove that you can do what a man can or even better is unnecessary. Or trying to prove that you don't need a man or you are the new male is pointless. We have women forsaking their uniqueness, to look and sound masculine. A woman can be strong and powerful yet nurturing, compassionate, and sensitive to the needs of others around her, just the way she was created to be—feminine.

Increasingly, we are seeing men dressing and behaving feminine even when they are straight. And women acting masculine even when they are straight. We have men being discouraged from being too masculine. Men, by design, will be masculine unless dumbed down to think and act otherwise. The spirit of Jezebel is attempting to flip the roles of the genders and make men into Ahabs to matriarch the social norm.

The Counsel of Balaam

Balaam counseled the king of Moab to use women as a weapon to cause a blessed nation to come under a curse, and the counsel worked. The men of Israel were bewitched, drawn away from Yahwah into worshipping a pagan deity. Balaam's false prophetic voice created a stumbling block, resulting in an apostasy and a plague which killed 24,000 men. Women of God, I challenge you to arise in prayer and intercession so that our men are not bewitched, annihilated, or feminized and come under God's curse.

The enemy's strategy now is the same as it was then: use women, who do not mind using their sexuality as a weapon and their mark of dominance. When women use their sexuality to have their way, it's witchcraft. Anything that has the power to manipulate the will of another, whether by force or seduction, is witchcraft. The incident at Baal Peor falls under witchcraft because women used their bodies, sensuality, and sex as tools to manipulate men into abdicating their positions as rulers and leaders, to become irresponsible individuals governed by sexual gratification.

"Baal Peor" means *breach or Lord of the openings*. The incident at Peor created a breach where covenant existed, to prevent a nation from crossing over into its promised land. People are able to cross over from promise to fruition, from prophecy to fulfillment, because they kept the covenant. They were faithful. Covenant in marriages are breached through lust, porn, infidelity, and other forms of immorality. Israel encountered the same situation at Peor just as they were about to enter the Promise Land. Oftentimes, the enemy sends his agents to attack covenant relationships; men working with women and women working with men on godly assignments and in society as a whole just before they are about to fulfill their prophetic destiny or move to a higher level.

The church is at a place where men and women are arising to take their individual places and together fulfill their roles not only within the four walls of the building but in society as a whole; but I discern the spirit of Jezebel wanting to create a breach, to create a Peor situation in this covenant relationship. Thus, creating a matriarchal culture in and outside of the church. United, in covenant, male and female can prevent the flip from happening.

Reflection

1. Am I fulfilling my role as a diplomat sent from God on a specialized mission to earth?
2. Am I in the habit of inspecting my life for breaches and openings that can give demons access?
3. Am I one who keeps covenant?

Prayer and Declaration

Male and female created he them; and blessed them, and called their name Adam. Father, we stand in agreement with your design and purpose for both genders. You called them, mankind. You created us equal. I pray that your people will recognize and embrace the equality and honor you placed on both genders so that we work in peace and covenant, not falling into Satan's trap of dominating each other. Father, let there be no breach among us, but heal and unite us, in Jesus' name. Amen.

Chapter 9:

Defeating the Demon of Witchcraft

Setting Boundaries and Defining Relationships

We often begin relationships, expecting those we connect with to conduct themselves in a reasonable, responsible manner and on many occasions, we are disappointed. Thus, it becomes important to define relationships which will result in boundaries being established.

Those You Are Connecting With

Always clearly state why you are connecting with someone; what you expect to receive and give and what privileges and access may be exchanged. It's wise to establish this at the beginning of the relationship instead of waiting until the relationship has progressed, since it may be uncomfortable to do so later.

Those Connecting with You

If someone is desirous of connecting with you, find out what their expectations are. Most people usually want something, even if they don't say it from the beginning.

Family and Friends

Even amongst family and close friends, it may become necessary to establish boundaries, especially if they are behaving in a manner you find unacceptable.

The Workplace

Although I have not singled out this area directly, the workplace is one of those places where we encounter unprecedented witchcraft attacks. People can push boundaries even if you have set them. Consequently, you need to remain firm, get superiors involved if necessary, document communication concerning violations, and know the company's guidelines regarding how employees on every level should interact with each other. Refuse to be dominated. Ensure your rights are respected.

Church Leaders

Too often we hear about hurt and abuse of church members but rarely do we hear about the hurt and abuse of church leaders because leaders often suffer in silence. Leaders, not everyone should have equal access to you. You don't have to tolerate abusive people or Jezebelic people. Feel free to ask them to move on. Surely, your church is not the only one in the country. And no, you don't have to roll out a welcome carpet for troublesome people who left and now try to come back. It's better for everyone if they stay gone!

Of course, the church is a place for the broken, but you cannot help the broken if you are broken yourself. Church leaders suffer from stress, depression, and all sort of ailments because they are afraid to say "no" out of the fear of being judged or of being accused of not being loving. Thus, we have people in the church behaving in a manner that they would never dare to behave on their jobs, because church people view the tolerance of unacceptable behavior as a show of love. Remember, the Scripture admonishes us to love our neighbor as ourselves. When you allow people to abuse and misuse you, you are not loving yourself.

When Dealing with Witchcraft Attacks

Don't fight in the flesh: Do not fight a fleshly battle. The spirit of witchcraft is a manifestation of the work of the flesh. Thus, attacks are assigned to trigger a carnal response from you. You cannot defeat the enemy using tools from his own arsenal. Jehu was the commander who God had anointed king over Israel. He was tasked with executing God's judgment on Jezebel. Let's look at how Jezebel tried to trigger a fleshly response from Jehu and how he handled it.

"Now when Jehu had come to Jezreel, Jezebel heard *of it;* and she put paint on her eyes and adorned her head and looked through a window. Then, as Jehu entered at the gate, she said, '*Is it* peace, Zimri, murderer of your master?' And he looked up at the window, and said, 'Who *is* on my side? Who?' So two *or* three eunuchs looked out at him. Then he said, 'Throw her down.' So they threw her down, and *some* of her blood spattered on the wall and on the horses; and he trampled her underfoot." (2 Kings 9:30-33 NKJV)

Jezebel taunted Jehu, but Jehu completely ignored her and focused on engaging those who would aid him in destroying her. The wisdom from this is, "Don't dialogue with what you were assigned to destroy."

Put on the armor of God: "Put on the whole armor of God, that you may be able to stand against the wiles of the devil." (Ephesians 6:11 NKJV)

Pray: This will get you supernatural assistance, strength, and strategies.

Worship: This is one of the most powerful weapons of war. "*Let* the high praises of God *be* in their mouth, And a two-edged sword in their hand, To execute vengeance on the nations, And punishments on the peoples; To bind their kings with chains, And their nobles with fetters of iron; To execute on them the written judgment—This honor have all His saints. Praise the Lord!" (Psalms 149:6-9 NKJV)

Bind and loose: Bind the spirit behind the attacks and loose freedom, victory, and liberty over yourself.

Use the blood of Jesus: There is power in the blood of Jesus. The blood of Jesus has already redeemed you from the works of domination of the enemy.

Use the Word of God: Read, meditate on, and fill your mind with things God has said about you. Witchcraft will attack your identity but you can maintain it by staying in the Word.

Decree and declare the written and prophetic Word: It is always good to remind yourself concerning what God has said about you. Make prophetic words into declarations and speak them over your life. By doing this, you come into agreement with heaven, thus breaking the heaviness of witchcraft.

Use the name of Jesus: This is the name by which every knee shall bow. During an attack, speak the name of Jesus more that you speak the name of your attacker.

Love: Loving our enemies gives us power over any fleshly reaction thus, preventing us from self-destructing in the midst of warfare.

Bless: Don't fight witchcraft with witchcraft. Don't pronounce curses on those the devil is using against you. Cursing is a manifestation of witchcraft. Bless your enemy; it's like building a muscle. It's painful and takes a lot of courage at first, but after a while, you will do it effortlessly. Blessing your enemy helps you maintain your posture of power and authority.

Break soul ties: A soul tie forms when your mind, will, and emotions become linked to another person whether under good circumstances or bad. Soul ties, especially with witchcraft personalities, form during good times, thus they begin as a channel through which love, intimacy, ideas, and connectivity flow. When the dynamics of the relationship shift to one of manipulation and intimidation, the soul tie becomes evil and consequently, a channel for demonic oppression and control. An evil soul tie will prevent forward momentum; thus, it has to be broken. Here is a simple prayer you can say to break evil soul ties:

"Father, in the name of Jesus, I break the soul tie between myself and…I declare that I am free of their influence and control. I close every channel in my mind, will, and emotions that existed between us. I cast down vain imaginations and flashbacks associated with that unpleasant season of my life. In the name of Jesus, I decree that I am free to move forward into my destiny."

Jezebelic Personalities

Jezebelic personalities oftentimes either struggle to recognize that they have a problem or they are too proud to acknowledge that they need to repent of their ways. Therefore, in order to preserve our sanity and destiny, we need to set boundaries and even remove ourselves from a relationship with such individuals. However, I do not believe that such individuals are outside of the reach of God's love and convicting power. I believe that such individuals can experience total freedom if they are willing to humble themselves and seek the necessary counseling and deliverance, and find themselves in a church community in which they can be effectively disciple.

Jehu and Jezebel the Principality

The spirit of Jezebel relies on the use of illegitimate authority. This spirit disregards and overrides the will of others to impose its will and desires. In 2 Kings, God anointed Jehu as king over his people and gave him the assignment to destroy Ahab's demonic dynasty, and Jezebel along with it.

"Then he arose and went into the house. And he poured the oil on his head, and said to him, 'Thus says the Lord God of Israel: "I have anointed you king over the people of the Lord, over Israel. You shall strike down the house of Ahab your master, that I may avenge the blood of My servants the prophets, and the blood of all the servants of the Lord, at the hand of Jezebel. For the whole house of Ahab shall perish; and I will cut off from Ahab all the males in Israel, both bond and free."'" (2 Kings 9:6-8 NKJV)

Jehu's kingly anointing speaks of the apostolic anointing. Every prophet is apostolic and every apostle is prophetic. In fact, every born-again believer carries a kingly anointing, Revelation 1:6 says, "And has made us kings and priests to His God and Father, to Him *be* glory and dominion forever and ever. Amen." (NKJV) However, just because you carry a kingly anointing doesn't mean you must fight a battle not assigned to you. You may not have the grace for it; but if Jezebel brings witchcraft to your doorstep, you need to fight.

Jehu was assigned to strike down Ahab's house. Even though the majority of evil deeds done during his reign were at the hands of Jezebel, his wife.

When God spoke a word of judgment, it was first against Ahab—man of the household and king of the nation. There is a price to pay for not walking in your God-assigned authority, thus permitting evil to prevail in situations in which you could have influenced righteousness to prevail.

Every apostle and prophet is anointed to strike down Ahab's house which are those systems and ideologies that oppose the standard God has set for his people, and those systems that oppress the believer. Apostles and prophets both carry the anointing to build God's people and by extension, his Church. Before any structure is built, opposing structures and systems need to be struck down and removed to the point that they will never rise again or impact the future of the saints. This is the reason all of the males in Ahab's bloodline had to be destroyed. The Church cannot and must not coexist in or with a Jezebelic system. One will destroy the other.

We still have situations in which apostles and prophets remain in their separate quarters; each trying to keep his tights, cape, and crowd intact, each trying to be a superhero in his own circle. Thus, some apostles try to flow like prophets, therefore, they don't need prophets. And some prophets vacillate between the two offices; one week they are a prophet, the next they are an apostle, creating unnecessary confusion. This is the reason Jezebel remains enthroned. Although Jehu was the king assigned to unleash the wrath of God on Jezebel, he did not allow himself to be overcome by the superhero syndrome.

The destruction of Jezebel has to be a team effort. "And he looked up at the window, and said, 'Who *is* on my side? Who?' So, two *or* three eunuchs looked out at him. Then he said, 'Throw her down.' So they threw her down, and *some* of her blood spattered on the wall and on the horses; and he trampled her underfoot." (2 Kings 9:32-33 NKJV)

Jezebel's Demise

Jezebel was proud and pompous to the end. People with Jezebelic personalities rarely let go of their self- important mindset. However, Jezebel was thrown down, because God's prophetic voice spoke a word of judgment against her. The current Jezebelic world system that is seeking to impose its will on the people of God will be thrown down like its wicked queen.

God is rising up a prophetic generation that will release a unified utterance against the Jezebelic world system and its witchcraft. The collapse of the system will be final with absolutely no memorial.

"So they went to bury her, but they found no more of her than the skull and the feet and the palms of *her* hands. Therefore, they came back and told him. And he said, 'This *is* the word of the Lord, which He spoke by His servant Elijah the Tishbite, saying, "On the plot *of ground* at Jezreel dogs shall eat the flesh of Jezebel; and the corpse of Jezebel shall be as refuse on the surface of the field, in the plot at Jezreel, so that they shall not say, 'Here *lies* Jezebel.'"' (2 Kings 9:35-36 NKJV)

The wicked queen who murdered God's prophets, deprived the innocent of their rights and drove terror in the heart of the Elijah was reduced to a skull, and palm of hands and feet. Everything else had been eaten by dogs. I am closing with this poem:

> O how the mighty has fallen, has fallen.
> Jezebel the Great has fallen.
> The whore who ruled the nations and terrorized God's people has fallen.
> There will be no memory of her.
> No one will shed a tear for her.
> The earth will be free of her abominations.
> The nations will rejoice and sing for joy.
> Only these three remain as warning symbols of a coming judgment: skull, palms, and feet.
> Only these three remain as a sign that Jezebel will once again be thrown.
> Fallen, removed from the high places.
> The wonder who ruled the nations is no more.
> Jezebel has been thrown down, fallen.
> Dislodged, displaced, destroyed.
> Destruction is certain for the Whore of Babylon.

Reflection

1. Am I someone who sets and maintains boundaries with those in relationship with me?
2. Do I worship in the midst of warfare?
3. Am I always conscious of the fact that I am anointed to strike down Ahab's house?

Prayer and Declaration

Father, in the name of Jesus, I pray you will cause to arise a mighty army, who with great might, will strike down Ahab's house. An army that will pull down the principality of Jezebel from its high place and establish your kingdom on the earth.

Acknowledgments

I would like to acknowledge the following people who helped to make this project possible:

Anil Katchon
Barbara Cocks Ejingiri
Celestine Lancer
Donna De Monick
Eunice Jubitana
Gene Coates
Gino and Marisha Olivacce
Kerry Laurence
Richard Tjin Asjoe
Sheraiva Welch
Sherida Mak
Sophia Brown
Steven Smeins

Thank you so much for your support!

About the Author

Prophetess Rhonda Amsterdam is the co-founder of *The Brook Place – St Maarten*, along with her husband, Claude. She is also the founder of *The Brook Place Prophetic Academy*, an online prophetic training hub. She is an ordained prophet, a wife, and mother of Kesha, Daniel, and Nathan. She resides in the Netherland Antilles.

Contact the Author

Facebook: Rhonda Amsterdam & Prophetess Rhonda Amsterdam
Instagram: Rhonda Amsterdam
Email: rhondaamsterdam2@gmail.com
Telephone: 1 721 550 4939